The International Wine and Food Society's Guide to

sweet puddings and desserts

by Margaret Sherman

with an introduction by
Keith Fenwick Bean

Other Books in the Series

The International Wine and Food Society's Guide to

puddings

and desserts

colour photographs by Kenneth Swain

The International Wine and Food Publishing Company

 DAVID & CHARLES

A publication of
The International Wine and Food Publishing Company
Marble Arch House, 44 Edgware Road, London, W2

This book was designed and produced by
Rainbird Reference Books Limited
Marble Arch House, 44 Edgware Road, London, W2

Indexer: Dorothy Frame

ISBN 0 7153 5177 X

Printed in Great Britian by
A. Wheaton & Co., Exeter

By the same Author

The International Wine and Food Society's
Guide to EGGS

For Shirley and Nicola–Jane

contents

American equivalents of English measurements are included, where necessary, in brackets.

colour plates

acknowledgements

Special appreciation to Margaret Robinson Sneade who—from start to finish, as with my earlier book on EGGS—has been my practical and expert critic.

Some recipes evolved from my job as hostess editor of *Good Housekeeping* magazine and I am grateful to the National Magazine Company for access to recipes tested by its Institute and to my colleagues there, Margaret Coombes and Mari Escritt.

Gillian Porter did a sterling job at her typewriter. Finally, my thanks to my husband, Keith Fenwick Bean without whose help this book would not have been written.

introduction

The rich offerings of puddings and desserts in this book are sweets in the menu sense, not the confectioner's shop sense. They include sweetmeats but not meat puddings. They are colloquially 'afters' or, more voguishly, 'finishers'.

Pudding, as a word, is something of a mystery. Dessert is simple – from the French *desservir*, to take away what has been served, the clearing of the table after dinner. Then came the fruit and sweetmeats. But, except that it first appeared in the twelfth century, the beginnings of the word pudding are obscure. Some have sought them in the old English stem *pud* (to swell) but there is no certainty that swelling had anything to do with the original meaning. Our pudding seems related to French *boudin* but the derivation of that is uncertain too. Wherever it came from, the English word in its current sense gives rise to modern French *pouding* and similar words in Dutch, German, Swedish, Irish and Gaelic.

In early days a pudding was boiled in a bag – either a cloth or some interior tubing from pig, sheep or other animal. Then the meaning spread to things boiled or steamed in a bowl covered with a cloth and later still to baked and fried dishes and to chilled puddings.

The things we eat in sweet puddings and desserts have their origins far back – in the earliest berries and nuts man picked and tried as food, in the first bird's nest and bee colony he ravished and the first wild grass seeds or acorns he soaked or pounded to make them eatable.

Milk of course is the first food man takes. It has always been highly regarded and Hippocrates was one of a long line of doctors to recommend it. Because it comes warm from the breast it may well have conditioned our ancestors to prefer heated foods in the beginnings of cooking.

Man's discovery that cereal grains can hold their vitality from year to year probably accounted for the mysticism which was early attached to them. Rice very soon had religious significance in India and China and still

11

retains it – and we have an echo of it in European and American wedding rice. Greeks, Syrians and Egyptians worshipped their goddesses of the corn and women who ceremonially feasted on pastries in the shape of male and female organs were not queerly indulging passion but seeking to promote the earth's fertility by magic.

The Scandinavian Yule rams and Yule goats were similarly inspired. Baked at Christmas, they were kept until sowing time. Then, to ensure good crops, the farm people ate them, fed some to the plough oxen and mixed some with the seed corn. Druidical worship is seen as the origin of rituals and divinations by cakes, apples and nuts among the Scots, Irish and Welsh. Yes, the Scots too – at any rate in the way the word druidical was used by eighteenth-century Scots writers and notably by John Ramsay, laird of Ochertyre, patron of Burns and friend of Sir Walter Scott. Around the May-day Beltane fires bits of cake were thrown, with suitable incantations, to the spirits – to encourage the protectors and appease the destroyers of flocks and herds.

Something more is implicit in the religious concept, not peculiar to Christianity, of transubstantiation. In ancient Mexican ceremonial the faithful took in something of the quality of the god Vitzilipuztli by eating him as a mixture of beet seed, maize and honey. Presumably some idea like this was also behind the practice sanctioned by Inquisition decree in 1903 of printing images of the Madonna and Child on soluble substances which could be fixed to sweetmeats and eaten.

Flour or meal was ground from wild grain before 9000 B.C. Cultivation developed later, some time in the next two thousand years. Cultivation spread from the warmer lands, even penetrating the Arctic circle. Wheat flourished early in the crescent from Anatolia through the Tigris and Euphrates valleys to the Nile. The quicker-ripening rye, barley and oats were more useful in the colder north. Rice, natural in the wet tropics, was eaten in India as early as 3600 B.C. and in China about 2800 B.C. Maize or Indian corn had to await Europe's discovery of the Americas before it crossed the Atlantic.

The sweetening in puddings and desserts in ancient times was honey. Many classical references from Homer onward show the high esteen in which it was held. The Syrians poured libations of it when they sacrificed to the sun. The voice in the burning bush promised Moses a land flowing with milk and honey. Honey was said to bestow long life on the ancient Corsicans and exemption from sickness on the Pythagoreans. In India it was used for preserving fruit.

Sugar cane, originating in the South Pacific, had by 500 B.C. reached India and China. In these countries people boiled down its juice to make sugar and treacle – which the Greeks called 'the honey of reeds' and 'honey not made by bees'. But quite early the Greeks knew it in crystallized form, too, and called it 'Indian salt'. Cultivation of cane spread, first to Persia and the Arab lands. By the thirteenth century England's wealthiest homes were buying it regularly, though only in small quantities because the price was extremely high – over £10 ($24.00) a lb. at today's values. More sugar came from expanding trade and new plantations and England took its full share. In 1598 a visiting German, Paul Hentzner, remarked on Queen Elizabeth's black teeth, 'a defect the English seem subject to, from their great use of sugar'.

It was not until the eighteenth century that sugar was established as a cheap food. It was then too that extracting sugar from beets began and eventually beet sugar became a factor in keeping supplies up and prices down. In the last 200 years Britain's annual consumption per head of sugar has increased twenty-five-fold to over 120 lb.

The European discovery of another pudding ingredient, cocoa, came with the voyages of Columbus and Cortes. The Aztecs had been growing it long before then, using it as a cold drink flavoured with vanilla. At first Europeans took it like soup, with hot spices. It reached England apparently about 1650 and, said to be a sex stimulant, soon became a rage. Samuel Pepys' diary records his approval of his first taste of 'jucalette', by that time a sweet drink. Eating chocolate developed commercially only in the nineteenth century.

Chilled sweets are much older. The ancient Chinese and then the Indians, Persians and Arabs made flavoured ices and sherbets. They stored snow or ice in underground pits, which acted as freezers – as the Greeks and Romans and, up to artificial ice-making, the English did. Marco Polo brought back to Italy a recipe for milk ices from his thirteenth-century Far East travels. He said the Chinese had been enjoying them since 3000 B.C. Ice creams were served at the royal court of France from the early sixteenth century and of England a hundred years later. The first English printed recipe seems to have appeared about the middle of the eighteenth century but it was not until the 1860s that ice creams were made commercially in Britain.

The first puddings were perhaps more like porridge, grain soaked in water until it swelled to bursting. When cooking began we can only guess. Boiling presumably had to await the discovering or invention of cooking vessels. Soaked hulled wheat was the basis of the very old and nourishing frumenty – a national dish in Britain in medieval times and still a tradition in some country kitchens. Baked or boiled in milk with sugar or honey, cinnamon and sometimes eggs, it makes a good dessert with fruit and cream. In Suffolk it was eaten, particularly through the twelve days of Christmas and some was left outside the door for the fairies. There is a family resemblance to frumenty in another old dish, hasty pudding, which goes back to Shake-speare's day at least. Originally a thick porridge of oats or barley, the name nowadays often applies to puddings made with tapioca, sago, semolina or flour.

Pottage, gruel, porridge, cake, pudding – historically they are often hard to distinguish. The Spartans of the seventh century B.C. enjoyed a porridge made from mixed seeds boiled in grape syrup, boiled wheaten groats and honey. Many ancient Greek cakes sound more like our puddings. A boiled one was of dough, honey, dried figs and walnuts. A dough fritter was boiled in olive oil and soaked in honey. Fritter fingers were of wine and lettuce juice, flour and pork fat. Other 'cakes' like the 'cakes' mentioned in Jeremiah (7:18), again in the seventh century B.C., were certainly pan-baked cakes. Baked puddings had rich sauces inside them. There were milk puddings, too, blancmange and milk-and-honey curds in moulds. One pudding St Paul must have eaten was made with milk, meal cakes and honey.

The Romans, like the Greeks, included many fresh fruits in their sweet dishes but they had many cooked sweets, too. Roman writers give instructions on reducing wine and must for sweetening sauces and preserving fruits. They also give recipes for fruit stews, stuffed dates cooked in honey, sweet-wine cakes steeped in milk and baked, fried bread-and-milk pudding, custards, custard tarts, sweet omelettes and iced sweets (cooled in snow).

The eating of puddings and desserts as 'afters' derives from the English adoption in the eighteenth century of the French fashion in the arrangement of courses. The habit began with the rich but by the end of the century inn and tavern meals quite commonly finished with a sweet dish such as rice pudding, gooseberry pie or tart. Sweet dishes continue to appear at earlier stages – melons, papaya or fruit juices to begin, fruit jellies, peach or pineapple or bananas with roast or fried savoury things, Chinese and other sweet-and-sour dishes. Sweetened sherbets and liqueurs still separate the main courses in major dinners.

In much the same way the ancient Macedonians, Greeks and Persians would have sweets in more than one course and might interrupt more elaborate feasts for sessions of drinks and desserts. In some parts sweet dishes were served before dinner, which the noted physician, Heracleides of Tarentum, argued was better because on a full stomach they could 'cause winds and fermentation'.

Desserts nevertheless normally came at the end of the meal. They accompanied the symposium which means, literally, the drinking together and was the after-dinner drinking bout. That is presumably why they included what might be called 'blotters-up' like boiled chick-peas, beans, pulses, nuts, myrtle berries, arbutus berries and edible acorns among the cheesecakes, pastries, puddings, eggs, bonbons, and fresh and dried fruits.

The dessert-and-drinks session was often elaborate, introduced with grace and ceremony and enlivened with music and other entertainment. The slaves cleared the tables and brought water (for the guests to wash their hands), perfumes, garlands and incense. Archestratus, a contemporary of Aristotle and described as 'the inventive genius of cookery', speaks of after-dinner toasts and perfuming and adds: 'Crown the head at a banquet with chaplets of all the myriad flowers wherewith earth's happy floor doth bloom and dress the hair with fragrant distilled unguents, and on the soft ashes of the fire throw myrrh and frankincense. . . .' Sometimes the chaplets were of gold, a gift from the host who – like Cleopatra, copying the Romans – might also give his guests the precious perfume pots, drinking cups and platters from which they had dined.

The cabaret with the desserts was stag-party type. Apart from *hetaerae* and some entertainers the symposium was normally an all-male affair. The entertainments could range through philandering with the cup-bearers (boys as well as girls), bawdy songs and dances, naked girl jugglers, fire-eaters and musicians. Among the ancient Celts the guests indulged in armed combats – sometimes, unintentionally warming up, to the death.

In medieval London, at least as early as the twelfth century, cooks' shops sold a wide selection of pies and puddings. The cooks could buy fruit in St Paul's churchyard where the gardeners of the 'Earls, Barons, Bishops and Citizens' of London sold their masters' produce until, in 1345, they were moved on for making too much noise.

Banquet menus from the days of King Richard II – who in his reign, from 1377 to 1399, was rated the best trencherman 'of all christian kynges' – show sweet dishes scattered through the meal. They included almond creams and marzipan, pears in syrup, white-wine jellies, fritters, sweet custards with dates, figs, prunes and cheese in them and many tarts and pies of plain and puff pastry. Each banquet course usually ended with a 'sotelte' or subtlety which was originally an imaginatively moulded or sculpted sweet. Later these subtleties became so elaborate – representing battles and other drama-tic scenes – that they must have been at least as much for show as for eating.

For most townsmen in Shakespeare's day sweet pastries were an occasional treat. With sugar still a luxury, honey, mostly from home-kept bees, re-mained the main sweetener. No doubt many housewives were grateful to Sir Hugh Plat for giving in his *Delightes for Ladies* in 1602 a recipe for sweeten-ing flour without sugar. He sliced parsnips thinly, dried and pounded them and mixed them with twice their weight of fine wheat flour.

Sweet puddings grew more popular in the next hundred years. A French visitor, M. Misson, waxed quite lyrical about English puddings. 'Blessed be he that invented pudding for it is a Manna that hits the Palates of all Sortes of People', he wrote. Christmas pie he described as 'a great Nostrum . . . a most learned Mixture'. This pie was what we now call mince pie except that it included neats' tongues and chicken. Most recipes for our now-traditional

15

Christmas sweets – mince pies and plum puddings – contained meat up to the middle of the eighteenth century. Hannah Glasse's 1747 plum pudding recipe, for instance, takes 'a leg or a shin of beef'. But change was under way. Our present Queen Elizabeth has a recipe from King George I, on the throne from 1714 to 1727, for a meatless plum pudding and such recipes became the accepted version in the next hundred years.

The reason why sweet puddings generally were on the way up was that, as one writer put it, 'sugar came to be in the Possession of the very poorest Housewife where formerly it had been a great Rarity'. Cook books included more varied and richer sweet dishes and in 1770 appeared a book devoted almost entirely to them, Mrs Glasse's *Compleat Confectioner*.

Treacle, sugar in even cheaper form, was a valuable stand-by in the dark nineteenth-century days of recurrent poverty and hunger. Even when things improved, treacle and the new cheap jams and sweetened condensed milk maintained their popularity, not least for flavouring and sweetening puddings. At the other end of the gastronomic scale the nineteenth century saw Carême raise the arrangement of puddings and the creation of architectural set pieces in sugar and pastry to an extravagance rivalling the 'soteltes' of earlier centuries. In England Alexis Soyer produced even more flamboyant fantasies in monuments of meringue, icing, ice and jelly.

Sweet puddings and desserts can be good value as food when fitted into a balanced diet – which is a much better way to health than any feeding fad. Elementary attention can balance the diet not only with individual requirements in quantity but also in the proportions of the essential energy-producers, growth and repair foods, mineral elements and vitamins. Desserts are no exception. For instance, a rice pudding or bread-and-butter pudding made with milk and eggs and served with blackcurrant sauce or strawberries has practically everything.

Milk is one of the few foods (avocado pears and nuts are others) with significant amounts of all three nutrients – proteins, fat and carbohydrates. It is also good for vitamins, calcium and phosphorus. Dried milk can be quite as good, especially when the manufacturer has enriched it with vitamins and minerals. Eggs, even richer than milk in proteins and fat, add iron to the good qualities of milk. Eggs and milk are light on vitamin C but one can make that good from nuts and some fresh fruits with, topping the list, blackcurrants, redcurrants, soft fruits and citrus fruits.

The carbohydrate contribution of puddings comes mostly from cereals, sugar and dried fruits. Eating chocolate has up to sixty per cent carbohydrate and about thirty per cent fat. Weight for weight, pure fats like lard, dripping, olive and other vegetable oils give us about $2\frac{1}{2}$ times the energy we get from starchy and sugary foods. Butter, about eighty per cent fat, gives us twice as much. Cream has about half the fat of butter. Suet when bought already

16

shredded has up to sixteen per cent rice starch in it to keep the flakes separate.

Most fresh fruits in Britain give us more flavour than nourishment. Excepting bananas and white grapes, the carbohydrates their sugars provide are in small amounts and their minerals and B-complex vitamins are not very important. For vitamin A, however, apricots are very good and peaches, nectarines and tangerines quite good. Dried fruits like currants, dates, figs, raisins and sultanas are rich in available carbohydrates. Canned fruits retain much of their vitamin C, often more than fruit bought in urban shops and cooked at home. The food value of jams comes from the fact that they are by weight more than half sugar. The value of jellies similarly depends on the sugar they contain.

On health grounds both fruit and sugar have been subjected to prolonged attack. For centuries doctors regarded fruit as suspect. Chiefly responsible was Galen (born about A.D. 130) who declared his father lived to 100 by never eating fruit. In 1539 Sir Thomas Elyot still echoed Galen. 'All fruites generally are noyfulle to man', Sir Thomas wrote, 'and do ingender ylle humours and be oftetymes the cause of putrified fevers.' It was not until the eighteenth century that new medical thought began to kill off such ideas. Fortunately the layman does not always listen to his doctors.

Criticism of sugar has grown in proportion to our increasing use of it. But up to the 1970s at any rate, there was no universally accepted proof of any of the charges – even for the accusation that it contributes to dental decay. Sugar however does take the edge off appetite – so sweet things before or between meals can be bad if they cut down the intake of the protein and protective foods necessary to full health. There is thus solid reason for taking our puddings and desserts at the end of the meal. In Britain over half of us take them that way with our main meal on week days and over two thirds of us on Sundays.

And so to Margaret Sherman's lore and recipes with their promise of 'many a winding bout of linked sweetness long drawn out'. Or should we say 'a perpetual feast of nectar'd sweets where no crude surfeit reigns'?

Keith Fenwick Bean

some essentials

The function of puddings and desserts and their glory are achieved when something delicious gives a meal the rounding-off completeness of contentment. Today the dessert can be a wine-laced tropical fruit salad, a flaming Normandy omelette, a simple palate-freshening sorbet, a Carême-inspired architectural gâteau or one of those tradition-enshrined homely 'puds'.

Simple or elaborate, puddings and their enjoyment have a tradition as long as civilized eating. It was more than two thousand years ago that the poet, Pindar, observed, 'As the banquet draws to its close, sweet is dessert though it follows bounteous food'. But be the meal bounteous or not, the dessert should be wisely balanced and harmonized with it.

Definitions

Time and geography sometimes give rise to different uses of the same word. These recipes aim to give American usage where it differs from that most usual in Britain. A pie is thus a dish covered with pastry or other lid. An open-faced pastry sweet (often called a pie in America) is a tart or flan. A flan crust or case is a pie shell in America. Other British-American equivalents are listed at the end of the book. In the recipes, flour is plain wheat flour unless otherwise stated. Eggs are the 2-oz. size, the 'standard' egg in Britain and the 'large' in the United States. Double (heavy) cream has at least 48% butterfat, single (light) cream at least 18% – so single cream is normally too thin for whipping which requires 37% butterfat. Fruit is fresh fruit unless otherwise qualified. Sugar, unspecified, means granulated sugar and, for simplicity, I have used 'fine sugar' to mean Britain's caster sugar or, more colloquially, shaking sugar. For Americans this signifies granulated sugar though some of them may prefer the finer-ground grade called in the United States powdered sugar. Icing sugar in British usage is confectioners' sugar in American.

18

Measures

British standard measures, used in the recipes, are tabulated with American equivalents in brackets (where necessary) and metric equivalents are at the end of the book.

Temperatures

Simmering temperature is 205°F. (96°C.) and tepid about blood heat, 98°F. (37°C.). Sugar-boiling temperatures (the sugar first dissolved in water) range from 215°F.–310°F. (102°–154°C.) and a sugar thermometer is the accurate aid. Oven temperatures vary but descriptions, as a general guide, are:

	°F.	°C.	GAS MARK
Very slow oven	250–275	121–135	$\frac{1}{4}-\frac{1}{2}$
Slow	300	149	1–2
Warm	325	163	3
Moderate	350	177	4
Fairly Hot	375–400	191–204	5–6
Hot	425	218	7
Very hot	450–475	232–246	8–9

Flavourings

Essences, as used in the recipes, are the natural, not the synthetic, products. Many spices and other flavourings can be introduced to puddings and desserts by flavoured sugar, milk, flour or other ingredients. Vanilla sugar is white sugar stored in tight-lidded jars with a vanilla pod (or the pod can be infused in milk or water). Cloves and cinammon stick can be used in these ways too. Caraway seeds – 1 tablespoon ($1\frac{1}{4}$) to $\frac{1}{2}$ lb. (2 cups) flour – can go into steamed or baked puddings. Ground aniseed – 1–3 oz. to 1 lb. (2 cups) sugar – can flavour steamed or milk puddings and pastry. Pounded cardamom or coriander seeds can replace or complement spices like cinnamon or cloves in fruit dishes, mincemeat and pastry. For spicy overtones in a sauce try a teaspoon of ground cardamom seeds blended into a pint of honey, maple syrup or jam sauce. Poppy seeds go well in dessert sauces and glazes and in filling for pies, tarts and strudels. Use sesame seeds in the same way after warming them up in a frying pan with or without a little butter or oil. Flower flavourings and decorations are in chapter 11.

Wines for the sweet course

If the sweet dish is to be a crowning glory, then for special occasions, a wine to complement it deserves thought. There are wines that marry happily with most things, though puddings rich in chocolate, ice-cold sweets and uncooked pineapple tend to overwhelm most wines. While wines, liqueurs and spirits are integral to many delicious sweet recipes, they may or may not drink well as complements to them.

The most common partners will be the sweeter wines. For blander puddings the wines may have only a fleeting kiss of sweetness. For the richest offerings they will range into wines we might consider altogether too luscious when taken on their own or with unsweetened food. Raymond Postgate makes the point that if you keep the sauternes and barsacs for the end of the meal, with the fruit, 'their sweetness will be less cloying and your palate can attend to their almost childish series of scented flavours'. Although palates are as individual as fingerprints, this principle applies pretty widely.

The sweeter wines to go with desserts may be natural or fortified, still or sparkling. The world leaders, in my thinking, are those where the grapes' sugars have concentrated by long ripening and late harvesting and that mysterious multi-scented bouquet has been introduced by noble rot – the *pourriture noble* of France, the *Edelfäule* of Germany, the *Aszu* of Hungary. Chief among these are the finest sauternes (Château d'Yquem at the top, of course, and including the best barsacs) from Bordeaux, the rich hocks and moselles (from *Auslese* to *Trockenbeerenauslese*) from Germany and the great tokays (first *Aszu* and, in good years, *Szamorodni*) from Hungary. At their best they are expensive, naturally, but they have many more modest cousins from many countries which are quite reasonably priced. The same thoughts apply to the sparkling wines. There are others, besides the recognised champagnes, eminently suited to desserts – Asti Spumante from Italy, for instance, or a sparkling Vouvray of a year when the sun is kind to that part of the Loire.

Among the fortified wines there are not only the light ports and brown sherries but plenty to explore among the malmseys and buals of Madeira, the commanderia of Cyprus, the marsalas from Sicily and the malagas from Spain. In addition there are the mis-named *vins doux naturels*, mostly lighter on the palate, from the Mediterranean coast of south-eastern France.

steamed and boiled puddings

Civilization is founded on pudding. Yes, the point can be quite reasonably argued. Man's discovery that wild seeds could be made eatable by pounding and soaking led to his growing seeds deliberately. That increased his carbohydrates, on which primitive diet was probably light, but it had even greater significance for society. It permitted bigger settlements, for land under grain can give five times as much food as it yields from livestock. So those first cereals, thousands of years ago, contained the seeds of our modern cities.

Today some of the most satisfying puddings remain comparatively simple flour-based mixtures merely boiled or steamed.

Methods
Precisely, one 'steams' in a double-tiered steamer (double-boiler), with the base of the utensil half-filled with rapidly boiling water. Without a steamer, the pudding basin goes directly into a large pan with boiling water half the depth of the basin. Either way, the water must boil continuously throughout the cooking or the pudding will be sad and heavy, so have a kettle of boiling water ready to top up the pan water from time to time. The steamer or pan should have a tight-fitting lid.

A pudding is truly 'boiled' when it is totally immersed in water, as with plum duff, roly poly or spotted dick, traditionally wrapped like a football or a sausage in a pudding cloth. Some dumplings are dropped straight into boiling water with no covering or wrapping around them.

Preparing basins, moulds and cloths
For puddings cooked in a bowl, a plain bowl is easier to turn out, but fancy moulds can be used. Grease the container thoroughly with butter in readiness for the mixture or the pudding will be difficult to unmould. Fill the basin or mould not more than two-thirds full and even less for lighter mixtures. To cover the pudding mixture use buttered grease-proof paper and/or kitchen foil.

21

For duffs and the like, scald a pudding cloth in boiling water, wring it out and flour lightly the side that will be next to the pudding mixture. Spread the cloth in a bowl or basin to get a good shape. Pour or spoon the mixture in, seeing that the folds of the cloth are evenly distributed. Then, allowing room for the pudding to swell, gather up the ends and tie them securely, making a loop to fish it out when cooked. Stand the wrapped pudding on a plate in the pan, cover the pudding with boiling water and cook as indicated in the recipes.

Turning out puddings

Remove the basin or mould from the steamer or saucepan and, after a minute or so, remove the covering. Then, with the protection of pot holders or oven gloves, shake the mould slightly to bring the pudding away from the sides and slide a knife blade around it to make sure it will come away clean. Invert it on to a hot serving dish and carefully remove the mould. For a pudding cooked in a cloth, unwrap it carefully and slide it on to a hot serving dish.

STEAMED SUET PUDDINGS

The plain suet pudding is traditionally served with butter and brown sugar, but it is good too with a jam or syrup sauce (page 33) or fruit sauce (page 122). Use self-raising flour in the mixture and for increased lightness you can substitute up to half the self-raising flour with an equal weight of fresh breadcrumbs. For added richness, use a beaten egg and slightly less milk.

BASIC STEAMED SUET PUDDING

4–6 servings:

6 oz. (1½ cups) self-raising flour	**3 oz. (¾ cup) shredded suet**
pinch of salt	**about ¼ pint (full ½ cup) milk**
2 oz. (¼ cup) sugar	

Sieve the flour, salt and sugar into a bowl. Add the suet and mix well. Make a well in the centre and add enough milk to attain a soft dropping consistency. Put it into a greased 1½-pint (1-quart) pudding basin, cover with greased waxed paper or foil and secure it with a string. Steam it over rapidly boiling water for 1½–2 hours. Turn the pudding out on to a hot serving dish and serve hot.

FRUIT PUDDING

To the dry ingredients of the basic suet pudding add either 2 medium cooking apples, peeled, cored and chopped, and a little grated nutmeg, or 2 oz. (full ⅓ cup) chopped, dried apricots (soaked in water overnight), 1 medium chopped pear and grated rind of 1 lemon.

JAM OR SYRUP PUDDING

Put 2 tablespoons (2½) jam, marmalade, honey, golden syrup or treacle in the bottom of the greased pudding basin before adding the basic suet pudding mixture.

GINGER PUDDING

Add 1 teaspoon (1¼) ground ginger and ½ teaspoon (⅔) ground cinnamon to the dry ingredients of basic suet pudding and serve the pudding with custard sauce (page 66) or butterscotch sauce (page 34).

SUSSEX PLUM DUFF

Add to the basic steamed pudding ingredients 4 oz. (⅔ cup) each of currants and seeded raisins and 1 teaspoon (1¼) of ground cinnamon or mixed spice. Boil it in a cloth for 2 hours, unwrap and serve hot.

CLOUTIE DUMPLING

Cloutie dumpling is the Scots version of the plum duff – called cloutie because it is boiled in a clout or cloth. You can make it with the basic steamed suet pudding mixture but to be really traditional make it with 3 oz. (½ cup) oatmeal and 3 oz. (¾ cup) self-raising flour instead of 6 oz. (1½ cups) self-raising flour and moisten the mixture with a beaten egg and ale instead of milk. Boil for 2 hours, unwrap and serve hot.

SPOTTED DICK

Spotted Dick is less elegantly known also as spotted dog – which suggests poetic justice of some sort since Dalmatian dogs are sometimes called plum-pudding dogs.

23

For spotted Dick make a light version of the basic suet pudding mixture (page 22) – 3 oz. ($\frac{3}{4}$ cup) self-raising flour and 3 oz. (2 cups) breadcrumbs instead of 6 oz. ($1\frac{1}{2}$ cups) self-raising flour. Add 6 oz. (1 cup) currants to the dry ingredients and add only enough milk to give a fairly soft dough. Shape it into a roll on a floured board. Wrap it in greased waxed paper and then in foil, sealing the ends tightly, or tie it in a prepared pudding cloth. Steam it over rapidly boiling water for $1\frac{1}{2}$–2 hours or immerse it in boiling water and cook for 2 hours. Serve it with lemon-flavoured custard sauce (page 66).

PLUM PUDDING—1 (*Illustrated*)

Plum pudding in most countries means a pudding with plums in it but to the British and Americans it means the rich traditional climax to Christmas dinner – usually without plums, although some recipes include a few prunes. Because plum puddings improve with maturing they are made six or eight weeks in advance, and they are often made in quantity: a big one for Christmas and others to give away and to be enjoyed in the months after Christmas. There are almost as many recipes as there are cooks to use them. Quantities in the first recipe make three 2-pint ($2\frac{1}{2}$) puddings, or one 2-pint ($2\frac{1}{2}$) and four 1-pint ($1\frac{1}{4}$) ones. A 1-pint pudding ($1\frac{1}{4}$) should yield 6–8 servings. Serve plum pudding with brandy or rum butter or sauce (page 33), with zabaglione or syllabub (chapter 6) or with a plain white sauce (page 63) passed separately.

12 oz. (2 cups) raisins
12 oz. (2 cups) sultanas
12 oz. (2 cups) currants
2 medium apples, chopped
4 oz. (1 cup) chopped candied orange peel
4 oz. (1 cup) chopped candied lemon peel
6 oz. (1 cup) chopped blanched almonds
grated rind and juice of 1 lemon
$\frac{1}{2}$ pint ($1\frac{1}{4}$ cups) brandy or rum

$\frac{1}{2}$ pint ($1\frac{1}{4}$ cups) stout
8 oz. (2 cups) plain flour
$\frac{1}{2}$ teaspoon ($\frac{2}{3}$) ground ginger
$\frac{1}{4}$ teaspoon ($\frac{1}{3}$) powdered cloves
$\frac{1}{4}$ teaspoon ($\frac{1}{3}$) powdered cinnamon
$\frac{1}{4}$ teaspoon ($\frac{1}{3}$) grated nutmeg
$\frac{3}{4}$ lb. (3 cups) chopped beef suet
8 oz. (1 cup) fine sugar
6 oz. (4 cups) fresh breadcrumbs
6 eggs

Put all the prepared fruit into a large bowl. Add the candied peels. Stir in the almonds, the grated rind and juice of the lemon. Mix the brandy or rum with the stout and stir it into the fruit and peel mixture. Cover it and leave it for 24 hours.

Sift the flour and spices together and mix them with the suet, sugar and breadcrumbs. Beat the eggs, stir them into the fruit mixture and then gradually stir in the dry ingredients. Beat with a large wooden spoon until everything is thoroughly blended. Fill greased pudding basins three-quarters full with the mixture. Cover each basin with greased waxed paper and then a pudding cloth, tying the ends of the cloth to form a handle. Steam them for 7 hours, remove from the pans and let them cool. Leave the waxed paper in position but cover the basins with fresh cloths or foil and store them in a cool place to mature for 6–8 weeks. Then steam the pudding again for 6 hours on the day of using. Unmould it. Sprinkle it with warmed brandy or rum, set it alight and carry it flaming to the table – topped with a sprig of holly to keep away the witches.

PLUM PUDDING—2

Good and rich but simpler and smaller, this recipe from London's Good Housekeeping Institute makes enough for a 2-pint (2½) basin, giving 12–16 servings.

6 oz. (1½ cups) plain flour
1 teaspoon (1¼) mixed spice
½ teaspoon (⅔) grated nutmeg
3 oz. (2 cups) fresh white breadcrumbs
4 oz. (1 cup) shredded suet
4 oz. (1 cup) stoned raisins, chopped
8 oz. (1⅓ cups) currants

8 oz. (1⅓ cups) sultanas (white raisins)
1 medium cooking apple, peeled, cored and chopped
3 oz. (full ½ cup) demerara sugar
grated peel of 1 lemon
2 beaten eggs
½ pint (1¼ cups) strong ale

Sift together the flour and spices into a large mixing bowl. Add the breadcrumbs, suet, dried fruits, apple, sugar and lemon peel. Mix all well and stir in the eggs and ale gradually. Stir thoroughly and leave the mixture, covered, overnight. Turn it into a well-greased 2-pint (2½) bowl, cover with paper and cloth and boil for 6 hours or cook in a steamer for 8 hours. Re-boil for 3–4 hours before serving.

Traditionally the plum pudding goes to table veiled in blue flame. This is achieved by sprinkling the piping-hot pudding with warmed brandy or rum and setting the spirit alight. The best way to warm the spirit is to put 3 or 4

25

tablespoons of it into a well-warmed punch ladle. Since the alcohol is burned away the effect of this flaming, apart from the fun of it, is the residual flavour added. This added flavour is only marginal with a rich dish like plum pudding but with blander flamed (*flambé*) desserts it can be more important, sometimes decisive. A drier brandy or a white rum gives a more delicate flavour. More assertive additions come from the old fashioned 'fruity' red rums and, among the brandies, some of those from Spain, Italy or Germany.

SUET-CRUST PUDDINGS

Suet crust is, strictly, pastry but it can be rather tough when baked and is best used for boiled and steamed puddings. It is most important to use self-raising flour. This basic recipe makes enough to line a 1½-pint (1-quart) pudding basin, which will give 4–6 servings.

BASIC SUET CRUST

6 oz. (1½ cups) self-raising flour
½ teaspoon (⅔) salt

3 oz. (¾ cup) shredded beef suet
water to mix

Sieve the flour and salt into a bowl. Add the suet and mix well. Pour in the water, mixing with a round-bladed knife to give a light elastic dough. Draw it together with floured fingertips until it leaves the bowl clean and in one lump. Turn the dough on to a lightly-floured board, knead it lightly with the fingertips until it is smooth and roll it out to about ¼-in. thickness.

SUET-CRUST FRUIT PUDDING

Make the basic suet-crust dough (above). Cut off a quarter of it for the pudding's 'lid'. Roll the remainder into a circle twice the diameter of the top of a 1½-pint (1-quart) basin. Line the well-greased basin carefully with this circle and press it up to the rim of the basin with the fingertips. Closely pack in the chosen fruit (about 1 lb.) layered with sugar to taste, but do not add any liquid. Roll out the pastry lid and lift it, on the rolling pin, on to the top of the basin. Wet the edges of the dough and press them well together. Cut a square of greaseproof paper 4 in. larger than the top of the basin and grease it well. Make a 1-in. pleat down the centre of the paper and lay it over the basin, twisting and folding it round the edges. Then repeat the process with foil. Steam for 2 hours.

As for the fruit, cooking apples and pears should be cored, peeled and

26

sliced. Cut young rhubarb into 1-in. segments. Dried fruits like apricots, figs and prunes can be soaked overnight, drained and then added whole. Fresh peaches and nectarines are best peeled, stoned and sliced, but smaller fruits like plums, damsons, greengages and cherries give a better flavour if you don't remove the stones.

APPLE DUMPLINGS

4 servings:

1 basic suet-crust recipe
(page 26)
4 medium cooking apples

3 oz. (full ⅓ cup) fine or dark brown sugar

Roll out the dough and cut it in circles large enough to enfold an apple. Core and peel the apples. Stand an apple on each circle. Fill each apple centre with sugar. Draw up the edges of the dough, wet them and press them together firmly round each apple. Tie each apple in a damp floured cloth, immerse in boiling water and boil briskly for ½ hour. Serve with fresh cream.

STEAMED ROLY POLY

Roll out the basic suet crust into an oblong about 8 in. × 10 in. Spread it with jam, marmalade, syrup or mincemeat (page 57), leaving about ½ in. clear along each edge. Brush the edges with milk and roll up the dough, starting on a short side. Put it into a scalded and floured cloth and tie each end securely. Immerse it in a large pan of rapidly boiling water and boil for 2 hours. Unwrap it carefully and quickly and serve with appropriate sauce.

POTATO DUMPLINGS

In Prague I first tasted the sweet small dumplings called *Knedliky*. They were made with a light potato-flour dough enclosing, that time, fat black cherries. They were served in soup plates with lots of melted butter and we added ground cinnamon and sugar mixed together. These popular dumplings are Bohemian but abroad – in Hilder Gerber's *Cape Cookery*, for instance – are sometimes called Viennese dumplings. My recipe is for apricots but variations can include plums, damsons, soaked prunes, cherries or rhubarb. The potatoes must be of the floury kind.

APRICOT DUMPLINGS

6 servings:

1½ lb. boiled floury potatoes, hot	**pinch of salt**
	1 beaten egg
4–5 oz. (1–1¼ cups) plain flour	**1¼ lb. apricots**
walnut of butter	**fried breadcrumbs**

Put the potatoes through a ricer or a fine sieve. Cool them and mix in the flour, butter, salt and egg. On a floured board knead the mixture to a light dough, roll it out to about ¼-in. thickness and cut it into squares large enough to envelop an apricot. Split the apricots, slide out their stones and slip a sugar lump into each. When all are enclosed firmly in their squares of dough drop them into a large pan of lightly salted boiling water and boil 15 minutes. Remove them with a perforated spoon and, optionally, toss them in golden fried breadcrumbs. Serve immediately with melted butter, sugar and cinnamon.

DUMPLINGS WITH APPLE SAUCE (*Topfenknödel mit Apfelmus*)

The Austrians are fond of dumplings and *Topfenknödel mit Apfelmus*, dumplings with apple sauce, are favourites. Coated, as in my recipe, with golden butter-fried breadcrumbs, they look good and have the advantage of contrasting textures. The hot apple sauce served with them is, at its simplest, a sweetened thick apple purée (page 120) though it can be enlivened with a little cinnamon or other powdered spice. A purée of fresh plums is a popular alternative.

4 servings:

2 oz. (¼ cup) butter	**pinch of salt**
2 egg yolks	**grated rind of ½ lemon**
4 oz. (½ cup) cottage cheese	for fried crumbs:
3 tablespoons (3¾) double (heavy) cream	**2 oz. (¼ cup) butter**
	2 oz. (1⅓ cups) crumbs of stale white bread
4 oz. (2⅔ cups) fresh white breadcrumbs	**1 oz. (2 tablespoons) fine sugar**
2 oz. (½ cup) plain flour	

Beat the butter until soft and then beat in the egg yolks one at a time. Stir in the cheese, the cream and breadcrumbs. Sift the flour with the salt and add the lemon rind. Fold the flour into the other mixed ingredients and leave for 30 minutes. Shape it into dumplings. Poach the dumplings in simmering salt water for about 20 minutes.

Meantime, to prepare the breadcrumbs, melt the butter in a broad-based

28

pan and gently fry the crumbs until they are golden. Stir in the sugar. Drain the dumplings and toss them lightly in the fried crumbs. Serve at once with hot apple sauce.

STEAMED SPONGE PUDDINGS

What is important to remember with steamed sponge puddings is that they will rise considerably during cooking and that it is best to cook them comparatively gently. If you are putting the basin directly into water put an inverted saucer or small plate in the base of the saucepan to keep the direct heat away from the pudding mould. These puddings can be (and often are) cooked in the oven, standing in a bain-marie or other water container. By oven or top-of-stove method, where the whole is covered with a lid this is in fact 'steaming' rather than baking. Similar sponge mixtures, used for baked puddings, are discussed in chapter 3.

BASIC SPONGE PUDDING

4 servings:

4 oz. ($\frac{1}{2}$ cup) butter

4 oz. ($\frac{1}{2}$ cup) vanilla-flavoured fine sugar

2 beaten eggs

4 oz. (1 cup) self-raising flour

milk to mix

Butter a 1$\frac{1}{2}$-pint (1-quart) pudding bowl. Cream together well the butter and sugar and beat in the eggs a little at a time. Lightly beat in the flour and about 2 tablespoons (2$\frac{1}{2}$) milk until the mixture is smooth. Turn it into the basin, level off the surface, cover with buttered paper or foil and steam it for 1$\frac{3}{4}$–2 hours. Turn out of the bowl and serve with a jam sauce (page 33) or a fruit sauce (chapter 9).

HONEY SPONGE

For this Australian favourite omit the sugar from the basic sponge recipe and replace it with 3 tablespoons (3$\frac{3}{4}$) honey.

CHOCOLATE SPONGE PUDDING

Make a smooth paste of 1 oz. ($\frac{1}{4}$ cup) cocoa powder and 1 oz. (2 tablespoons) sugar with 1 tablespoonful (1$\frac{1}{4}$) hot water and add it to the creamed butter and sugar in the basic sponge pudding recipe. Then add 2 oz. ($\frac{1}{3}$ cup) chopped stoned raisins (optional) with the flour. Serve with rum sauce (page 33) or chocolate sauce (page 34).

29

MARBLE SPONGE PUDDING

Make up the basic sponge pudding recipe and divide it between two bowls.
To one, add the grated rind of 1 lemon and mix well. To the other add 1
tablespoon (1¼) cocoa powder. Spoon these mixtures alternately into a
greased 1½-pint (1-quart) pudding bowl or fluted mould (which gives the
marbled effect). Cover it and steam for about 2 hours. Unmould it, pour over
it lemon or orange sauce (page 122) and serve at once. One can vary flavours
and colours – with coffee and orange, for instance.

CANARY PUDDING

Add the finely grated peel of 1 lemon to the dry ingredients of the basic
sponge mixture (page 29). Serve with marmalade sauce (page 31) or a lemon
or orange sauce (page 122).

DELAWARE PUDDING

4 servings:

**1½ oz. (2 tablespoons) golden
  syrup**
1 canary pudding recipe
  (above)
**2 medium peeled, cored and
  sliced cooking apples**

2 oz. (⅓ cup) currants
**1 teaspoon (1¼) ground
  cinnamon**

Butter a 2-pint (1½-quart) pudding mould and put the syrup into the base.
Prepare the canary pudding mixture. Mix the fruit and spice together. Put a
thin layer of sponge mixture into the basin and then add alternate layers of
fruit and mixture, finishing with a thicker sponge layer on top. Smooth the
surface, cover with buttered paper and steam for about 1¾ hours. Unmould
carefully and serve with single (light) cream, brandy sauce or rum butter
(page 33).

ALMOND PUDDING

4–6 servings:

3 oz. (½ cup) ground almonds
**2 oz. (1⅓ cups) fresh white
  breadcrumbs**

1 basic sponge pudding recipe
**2 oz. (⅓ cup) chopped glacé
  cherries**

Mix the almonds and breadcrumbs with the flour in making the basic sponge
mixture and add sufficient milk (about 4 tablespoons) to give it a dropping
consistency. Mix in the cherries at the end. Steam 1½–2 hours and serve with

30

zabaglione (page 74) or custard sauce (page 66). Alternatively, substitute diced crystallized fruit and a little finely shredded orange and lemon peel for the cherries.

STEAMED BREAD PUDDINGS

Steamed bread pudding, fragrant with spices, full of currants and served with custard sauce belongs, for me, in my grandmother's kitchen. Hers was a recipe handed down from her grandmother. Other bread puddings, baked, appear in chapter 3.

CHERRY PUDDING

4 servings:

3 oz. (2 cups) brown breadcrumbs

1½ oz. (3 tablespoons) fine sugar

peel of ½ lemon, grated

6 oz. (1½ cups) stoned fresh cherries

½ pint (1¼ cups) double (heavy) cream

2 eggs, separated

for the sauce:

1½ oz. (3 tablespoons) sugar

3 oz. (¾ cups) fresh cherries

juice of ½ lemon

¼ pint (full ½ cup) water

Combine the breadcrumbs, sugar and peel in a bowl. Add the cherries. Scald the cream and pour it over this mixture. Beat the egg yolks and stiffly whisk the whites. Stir the beaten egg yolks into the cream mixture and then fold in the whites. Pour the mixture into a well buttered 1-pint (1½-pint) mould or bowl. Cover with buttered paper and steam gently for about 1¼ hours, until the pudding is well risen and firm to the touch. Meanwhile, make the sauce by bringing the remaining ingredients to the boil in a small saucepan, then reducing the heat and simmering for about 15 minutes. Unmould the pudding on to a hot serving dish, pour the sauce over it and serve immediately.

CHOCOLATE BREAD PUDDING

4 servings:

3 oz. (3 squares) semi-sweet
  chocolate
2 oz. (¼ cup) butter
½ pint (1¼ cups) milk
2 oz. (¼ cup) vanilla-flavoured
  sugar

2 eggs, separated
5 oz. (3⅓ cups) fresh white
  breadcrumbs
pinch of ground cinnamon

Melt the chocolate with the butter very gently over a pan of hot water. Add the warmed milk, sprinkle in the sugar and continue stirring for a minute or so. Remove from the heat. Separate the eggs. Put the whites aside and beat the yolks. Add the yolks and half the breadcrumbs to the chocolate and mix well. Stir in the remaining breadcrumbs and the cinnamon. Whisk the egg whites stiffly and fold them into the mixture. Pour the mixture into a well-buttered 2-pint (1½-quart) mould, cover with buttered paper and steam for 1–1½ hours, until the pudding is well risen and firm to the touch. Unmould and serve with custard sauce (page 66) or chocolate sauce (page 34).

SPICY BREAD PUDDING

4 servings:

2 eggs, well-beaten
¼ pint (full ½ cup) milk
1 teaspoon (1¼) powdered mace
1 teaspoon (1¼) powdered
  cinnamon
¼ teaspoon (⅓) saffron
¼ teaspoon (⅓) ground cloves
pinch of salt

3 oz. (full ⅓ cup) sugar
8 oz. (4⅔ cups) fresh white
  breadcrumbs
2 oz. (¼ cup) shredded suet
6 oz. (1 cup) currants
1 teaspoon (1¼) grated
  nutmeg

To the eggs add the milk, spices, salt, and nearly all the sugar; then mix in the breadcrumbs, suet and currants. When all is thoroughly stirred, leave it to rest for 30 minutes. Put it into a 1½-pint (1-quart) well-greased pudding basin and steam for 1½ hours. Unmould, dredge with nutmeg mixed with sugar and serve with custard sauce (page 66) or vanilla-flavoured white sauce (page 64). Optionally you can mix in a little brandy or other spirit with the breadcrumbs.

SAUCES FOR STEAMED PUDDINGS

Hard sauces, like rum butter or brandy butter, preserve the full value of the spirits rather than merely the residual flavours which are left when spirits are used in cooked dishes. Custards and custard sauces are in chapter 5, zabaglione, syllabub and other whipped sauces in chapter 6 and fruit sauces in chapter 9.

BRANDY AND RUM BUTTERS

For brandy butter: cream 3 oz. (full $\frac{1}{3}$ cup) butter until it is pale and soft. Gradually beat in 3 oz. (full $\frac{1}{3}$ cup) fine sugar. Add about 2 oz. ($\frac{1}{4}$ cup) brandy, a few drops at a time. The mixture should now be pale and creamy. Stiffen in the refrigerator before serving it. It is the chilling which gives these butters the name of hard sauces. For fuller flavour use Armagnac rather than cognac or, better still, a Spanish brandy. For rum butter: make this in the same way but use soft brown sugar, replace the brandy with $2\frac{1}{2}$ oz. (5 tablespoons) rum and add the grated rind of half a lemon. Again, the old-fashioned red and 'fruity' rums give stronger flavour than the white rums of more recent fashion.

BRANDY AND RUM SAUCES

Combine 3 egg yolks, 8 tablespoons ($\frac{1}{2}$ cup) double (heavy) cream, 8 tablespoons ($\frac{1}{2}$ cup) each of brandy (or rum) and water and 2 tablespoons ($2\frac{1}{2}$) sugar in a bowl over a pan of hot but not boiling water. Whisk until the sauce is thick and frothy. Do not let it boil.

JAM, SYRUP AND TREACLE SAUCES

To be served hot with steamed puddings, jam and syrup sauces are very easy. For jam or marmalade sauce add 2 oz. ($\frac{1}{4}$ cup) sugar and 2 tablespoons ($2\frac{1}{2}$) of jam to $\frac{1}{2}$ pint ($1\frac{1}{4}$ cups) water in a saucepan. Add $\frac{1}{2}$ oz. (1 tablespoon) arrowroot blended to a paste with a little cold water. Boil together for a few minutes and add lemon juice to taste. Strain and serve. For golden syrup or treacle sauces warm together 6 tablespoons (scant $\frac{1}{2}$ cup) water and 8 good tablespoons (full $\frac{1}{2}$ cup) syrup or treacle, stirring well. Simmer for a few minutes and then add the juice of half a lemon.

HOT CHOCOLATE SAUCE

Melt 2 oz. (2 squares) bitter chocolate in $\frac{1}{2}$ pint ($1\frac{1}{4}$ cups) water in a saucepan and bring to the boil. Mix 1 tablespoon ($1\frac{1}{4}$) of cornflour (cornstarch) to a paste with a little cold water and stir it into the pan. Stir in 2 oz. ($\frac{1}{4}$ cup) sugar and a pinch of salt; continue stirring until the sauce thickens and then about 3 minutes more. Remove it from the heat and stir in 1 oz. (2 tablespoons) butter and 2 tablespoons ($2\frac{1}{2}$) brandy or liqueur and a little finely grated orange peel (the brandy and the orange peel are optional).

BUTTERSCOTCH SAUCE

1 oz. (2 tablespoons) butter	**2 tablespoons ($2\frac{1}{2}$) golden syrup**
8 oz. (1 cup) brown sugar	**4 tablespoons (5) single (light) cream**

Warm the butter, sugar and syrup until they are well blended and add the cream. Bring to the boil and cook, stirring, for 3 or 4 minutes or until thick. Optionally, add 1 oz. (3 tablespoons) nuts, blanched and finely chopped.

baked puddings

One theory states that baked puddings began when our forefathers accidentally dropped a mash of water and coarsely ground wild grain in a camp fire, rescued it and liked the new flavour. Cooking doughs of flour or meal on a flat bakestone would follow naturally. Presumably the first results were a sort of bread – with flavour variations, sweetening, shortening and leavening coming later.

The refinements are now so many and varied that baked puddings spread through a good half of our dessert categories. Those here follow on from the steamed and boiled puddings in chapter 2 but others fall more naturally into later chapters. A baked soufflé omelette is included here among the soufflés, though other sweet omelettes are with the crêpes and other pan-made cakes in chapter 8.

BAKED SPONGE PUDDINGS

The sponge, with varying basic proportions of butter, eggs, sugar and flour, is ubiquitous. The sponge mixtures for steaming in chapter 2 are quite suitable for baking.

PLAIN BAKED SPONGE

4 servings:
1 basic sponge pudding recipe (page 29)

Put the mixture into a buttered ovenproof dish and bake it near the top of a moderate oven for 30–40 minutes until it is well risen and golden. Serve with fruit, an appropriate fruit sauce (page 122) or a jam sauce (page 33).

35

CITRUS SPONGE PUDDING

To the creamed basic mixture for plain baked sponge (page 35) add the grated rind of 1 orange or 1 lemon or a combination of both and use fruit juice instead of milk for mixing. Serve with a hot lemon or orange sauce (page 122).

SPICED SPONGE PUDDING

Sift $\frac{1}{2}$–1 teaspoon ($\frac{2}{3}$–1$\frac{1}{4}$) of mixed spice with the flour in the basic plain baked sponge recipe (page 35) and then add 3–4 oz. ($\frac{1}{2}$–$\frac{2}{3}$ cup) currants, sultanas or raisins and 1–2 oz. (about $\frac{1}{2}$ cup) chopped candied peel or glacé cherries to the flour. Serve with custard sauce (page 66).

GINGER SPONGE PUDDING

Add 2 pieces of preserved ginger, finely chopped, and about 2 teaspoons (2$\frac{1}{2}$) of ginger syrup to the basic mixture for plain baked sponge (page 35). Serve with a syrup sauce (chapter 2).

EVE'S PUDDING

The following recipe uses apples but cooking pears are a popular variation. Or try $\frac{1}{4}$ lb. blackberries and $\frac{3}{4}$ lb. apples or pears.

4–6 servings:

1 lb. cooking apples, peeled and cored
3 oz. (full $\frac{1}{2}$ cup) demerara sugar
grated rind 1 lemon

1 tablespoon (1$\frac{1}{4}$) water
1 plain sponge recipe (page 29), without the milk

Slice the apples into a buttered ovenproof dish, sprinkle them with sugar, lemon rind and water. Make up the plain sponge mixture but do not include the milk. Spread the mixture over the fruit. Bake it in the centre of a moderate oven for 30–40 minutes. Sprinkle it with fine sugar and serve hot with cream or with custard sauce (page 66).

LEMON LAYER PUDDING

This pudding separates in the cooking to give a lemon custard underneath and a light sponge topping.

36

4 servings:

2 oz. ($\frac{1}{4}$ cup) butter	2 eggs, separated
4 oz. ($\frac{1}{2}$ cup) sugar	$\frac{1}{2}$ pint ($1\frac{1}{4}$ cups) milk
grated rind and juice 1 lemon	2 oz. ($\frac{1}{2}$ cup) self-raising flour

Cream together the butter and sugar with the lemon rind to get the full benefit of the zest. Add the egg yolks and beat well. Stir in the milk, lemon juice and flour. Stiffly beat the egg whites, fold them into the mixture and pour into a buttered ovenproof dish of 2-pint ($1\frac{1}{2}$-quart) capacity. Stand it in shallow water in a baking tin and cook near the top of a fairly hot oven for about 45 minutes (until risen).

UPSIDE-DOWN PUDDINGS

Upside-down baked puddings, often called upside-down cakes in the United States, ask for a little artistry in arranging fruit or fruit and nuts in the base of the dish, since this part will be the topping when the pudding is turned out. Sweet sun-ripened fruits are obviously best, though most English recipes plump for bottled or canned fruits for their sweetness and regular shapes. Peeled, cored and sliced cooking apples or pears or rhubarb can of course be used and methods for cooking fresh fruits, including pineapple, are in chapter 9. Flavours can be varied not only with the fruits used but also by the addition of powdered ginger, cocoa or coffee, for instance, to the dry ingredients.

PINEAPPLE UPSIDE-DOWN (*Illustrated*)

4–6 servings:

for the topping:	4 oz. ($\frac{1}{2}$ cup) fine sugar
1 oz. (2 tablespoons) butter, melted	2 beaten eggs
2 oz. ($\frac{1}{4}$ cup) soft brown sugar	6 oz. ($1\frac{1}{2}$ cups) self-raising flour
pineapple rings	2–3 tablespoons ($2\frac{1}{2}$–$3\frac{3}{4}$) pineapple juice
for pudding mixture:	
4 oz. ($\frac{1}{2}$ cup) butter	

Use a square 7-in. 2-pint ($1\frac{1}{2}$-quart) ovenproof dish or a cake tin. If you use a tin put a square of buttered greaseproof paper in the base. Cover the base with the butter and sprinkle it evenly with sugar. (Alternatively, coat the base with golden syrup.) Arrange the pineapple rings decoratively over the base. Prepare the creamed mixture as for a plain baked sponge (page 35), using pineapple juice instead of milk. Spoon it over the fruit and spread it evenly. Bake it in the centre of a moderate oven for about 45–50 minutes.

Turn it out upside down on a warm serving plate. You can further decorate it with glacé cherries. Serve with a sauce made by thickening $\frac{1}{2}$ pint ($1\frac{1}{4}$ cups) of the fruit juice with 2 teaspoons ($2\frac{1}{2}$) arrowroot and adding 3 tablespoons ($3\frac{3}{4}$) of light rum.

BAKED CHARLOTTES

There are two kinds of charlottes – the cold *charlotte russe*, an invention of the great Carême which is detailed on page 81 (with an iced variant on page 93) and the much older baked fruit charlotte, served hot. Baked charlottes are made in a charlotte mould or a soufflé dish which is buttered, dusted with icing sugar and then lined with slices of white bread. The most traditional fruit filling is apple but it can equally well be plums, peaches, apricots, quinces, pears or rhubarb. The fruit must have a stiff consistency or it will soften the bread 'walls' and the charlotte will collapse when unmoulded.

The bread should not be too fresh, cut fairly thin (about $\frac{1}{4}$ in.) and with its crusts trimmed off. Each bit is dipped in melted butter. Cut triangles or hearts for the base and see that they cover it completely, slightly overlapping. For the sides, rectangular strips, the exact inside depth of the dish, can also slightly overlap; and then overlapping triangles (or a complete round from a large loaf) make the lid before the mould goes into the oven.

APPLE CHARLOTTE

4–6 servings:

for the mould:	**2 oz. ($\frac{1}{4}$ cup) butter**
melted butter	**4 oz. ($\frac{1}{2}$ cup) sugar, or to taste**
thin slices white bread	**juice and grated rind 1 lemon**
for the filling:	**pinch cinnamon**
$1\frac{1}{2}$ lb. cooking apples	**brown sugar**

Peel, core and slice the apples. Cook them in a heavy-based pan in the hot butter, adding the sugar, lemon juice, peel and cinnamon. Bring gently to the boil, stirring continuously with a wooden spoon. Lower the heat and simmer, still stirring frequently, until the mixture has thickened. Meanwhile line a charlotte mould or soufflé dish of $1\frac{1}{2}$-pint (1-quart) capacity as described above. Fill it right to the top with the apples. Put on its bread 'lid', first dipped in melted butter, and sprinkle the lid with brown sugar. Bake in a moderate oven for 35–40 minutes or until the bread is golden. Remove it from the oven and let it stand for some minutes before unmoulding it on to a warmed dish. Serve with whipped cream or apricot jam sauce (page 33) up-lifted with a little calvados.

BROWN BETTY

Close relative of the charlotte is the Betty – made with fruit and breadcrumbs or cake crumbs but cooked and served in a pie dish. Instead of the rhubarb in this recipe any fruit or fruit mixture can be used.

4–6 servings:

2 oz. ($\frac{1}{4}$ cup) butter	1 teaspoon ($1\frac{1}{4}$) powdered
1 lb. rhubarb	ginger or cinnamon
6 oz. (4 cups) fresh white	2 tablespoons ($2\frac{1}{2}$) golden
breadcrumbs	syrup
3 oz. (full $\frac{1}{3}$ cup) soft brown	1 tablespoon ($1\frac{1}{4}$) orange or
sugar	lemon juice
grated rind 1 lemon	1–2 tablespoons ($1\frac{1}{4}$–$2\frac{1}{2}$) water

Butter a 2-pint ($1\frac{1}{4}$-quart) pie dish. Put in a layer of rhubarb trimmed in short lengths. Mix together the breadcrumbs, most of the sugar, the rind and spice and layer alternately with fruit and crumbs, ending with crumbs. Heat the syrup with the fruit juice and water and when it is amalgamated pour it over the mixture. Sprinkle it with the remaining brown sugar, dot with butter and bake in a moderate oven for about 45 minutes or until the fruit is soft and the topping crisp and golden brown. Serve hot with cream.

As a variation, brown the breadcrumbs first in about 2 oz. ($\frac{1}{4}$ cup) butter and layer them with the fruit; add the zest and spice to the syrup.

SWEDISH APPLE CAKE

Layer browned crumbs with apple purée, making the first and last layers of crumbs. Dot the top with butter and bake near the top of a moderate oven for about 30 minutes. Serve warm with cream.

BAKED BREAD PUDDINGS

Like the summer puddings in chapter 9, bread-and-butter puddings are English desserts that tend to get lost along the line of keeping up with continental cuisine. Yet both are, at their simple best, very good and far from being just nursery fare.

BREAD-AND-BUTTER PUDDING

4–6 servings:

4 slices white bread
4 oz. ($\frac{1}{2}$ cup) butter
1 oz. (scant $\frac{1}{4}$ cup) currants
1 oz. (scant $\frac{1}{4}$ cup) sultanas

4 oz. ($\frac{1}{2}$ cup) sugar
3 whole eggs and 1 extra yolk
grated nutmeg
1 pint (2$\frac{1}{2}$ cups) vanilla-flavoured milk

Trim the crusts from the bread, butter the slices generously, cut them into strips and arrange them in a buttered ovenproof dish, buttered side up, sprinkling each layer with fruit and sugar. Beat the eggs and the extra yolk well with a little nutmeg and stir into them the warmed milk. Pour the mixture over the bread, grate some more nutmeg on top and leave it to stand for about 15 minutes. Bake it in the centre of a pre-heated moderate oven for about 40 minutes. Serve hot.

FRENCH BREAD PUDDING

4–6 servings:

5–6 oz. (3$\frac{1}{3}$–4 cups) fresh white breadcrumbs
3–4 oz. (full $\frac{1}{3}$–$\frac{1}{2}$ cup) sugar
1 pint (2$\frac{1}{2}$ cups) vanilla-flavoured milk

2 whole eggs and 3 extra yolks
2 egg whites, stiffly whisked
1 oz. (2 tablespoons) butter

Put most of the breadcrumbs in a bowl and stir the sugar into them. Boil the milk, pour it in and leave it for 15 minutes. Sieve the mixture. Beat the whole eggs and extra yolks and then beat them into the mixture. Fold in the egg whites and turn the mixture into a plain buttered mould lined with the rest of the breadcrumbs. Stand it in a baking tin of shallow water and bake it in a moderate oven for 35–40 minutes, until it is risen and pale gold. Serve hot with fruit sauce (page 122).

GERMAN BREAD PUDDING

Proceed as for the French version but substitute hock or moselle for the milk, use brown sugar instead of white and add a pinch of cinnamon. Serve with kirsh-flavoured or other liqueur-flavoured fruit sauce (page 122). Both this and the French bread pudding can also be steamed.

40

MIMI'S CARROT PUDDING

6–8 servings:

6 oz. ($\frac{3}{4}$ cup) **butter**	6 oz. (scant $\frac{2}{3}$ cup) **soft brown**
6 oz. (1 cup) **seedless raisins**	**sugar**
$\frac{1}{2}$ **lb. carrots.**	$\frac{1}{2}$ **teaspoon** ($\frac{2}{3}$) **grated nutmeg**
5 oz. (1$\frac{1}{4}$ **cups) self-raising flour**	$\frac{1}{2}$ **teaspoon** ($\frac{2}{3}$) **powdered**
pinch salt	**cinnamon**

Cream the butter. Chop the raisins, scrape and grate the carrots and stir all into the butter. Sift the flour and blend in the sugar, salt and spices. Combine these dry ingredients with the carrot mixture until malleable. Press the mixture into a buttered shallow baking dish. Bake in a warm oven for about 40 minutes. Serve warm, with cream.

QUEEN OF PUDDINGS

4–6 servings:

1 pint (2$\frac{1}{2}$ **cups) milk**	3 oz. (2 cups) **fresh**
$\frac{1}{2}$ **vanilla pod**	**breadcrumbs**
grated rind 1 lemon	3 tablespoons (3$\frac{3}{4}$) **strawberry**
1$\frac{1}{2}$ oz. (3 tablespoons) **butter**	**or black cherry jam**
2 oz. ($\frac{1}{4}$ cup) **fine sugar**	for the topping:
3 egg yolks	3 egg whites
	6 oz. ($\frac{3}{4}$ **cup) fine sugar**

Infuse the milk with the vanilla and lemon rind. Strain it, add 1 oz. (2 tablespoons) butter and the sugar. Whisk the egg yolks and add the warm milk to them, stirring vigorously. Strain the mixture over the breadcrumbs, pour it into a buttered pie dish and leave it for 10 minutes. Bake it in the centre of a moderate oven for 20–25 minutes, until just set. Remove it from the oven. Warm the jam and spread it over the custard mixture.

For the topping, whisk the egg whites stiffly and fold in the fine sugar. Pile the meringue on to the pudding in peaks, dredge them with sugar and return the dish to a moderate oven for 10–20 minutes until the meringue is lightly coloured and crisp-topped. Serve at once.

BAKED SOUFFLÉS

Soufflés have a quite undeserved reputation for being tricky to make. They are not. But they must go straight from oven to table for immediate eating to be at their best.

41

BASIC HOT SOUFFLÉ

4 servings:

1½ oz. (3 tablespoons) butter	pinch salt
1½ oz. (scant ⅓ cup) flour	4 egg yolks, well beaten
½ pint (1¼ cups) milk	5 egg whites
5 oz. (full ½ cup) fine sugar	

Butter a 7-in. soufflé dish of 2-pint (1½-quart) capacity. Melt the rest of the butter in a thick-based saucepan and stir in the flour until well blended. Add the milk and cook gently, stirring, until very smooth. Stir in the sugar and salt. Cool the mixture slightly and stir in the egg yolks. Meanwhile whisk the egg whites until they adhere peakily to the whisk. Fold them gently but thoroughly into the cooled mixture with a metal spoon. Pour the mixture into the soufflé dish, put it on a baking sheet in a pre-heated moderate oven and cook it until well risen and slightly coloured, about 30 minutes. Serve at once.

ALMOND SOUFFLÉ

Butter a 2-pint (1½-quart) soufflé dish and sprinkle it all over with crushed macaroons. Add a little almond essence to the initial egg-yolk mixture and proceed as for the basic hot soufflé above. With or without the macaroons, add 2 oz. (⅓ cup) finely chopped almonds to the soufflé mixture just before the egg whites.

CHOCOLATE SOUFFLÉ

Timing is important for chocolate soufflés, since the mixture may tend to dry out if over-cooked. Ideally they are crisp on top and creamy in the centre.

4 servings:

4 oz. (4 squares) bitter chocolate	3 oz. (full ⅓ cup) fine sugar
3 tablespoons (3¾) rum, brandy or water	4 egg yolks
	6 egg whites, stiffly whisked

Butter a 2-pint (1½-quart) soufflé dish. Melt the broken chocolate in a large bowl over hot water, stirring in the spirit or water. Stir until smooth and add the sugar. Beat in the yolks one at a time. Fold in the whites. Pour the mixture into the soufflé dish and bake it on a baking sheet in the centre of a pre-heated fairly hot oven for 18–20 minutes. Serve it with cream.

LIQUEUR SOUFFLÉ OMELETTE

4 servings:

6 eggs, separated
3 oz. (full ⅓ cup) fine sugar
grated rind 1 lemon or orange

2 tablespoons (2½) liqueur
½ oz. (1 tablespoon) butter
1 oz. (¼ cup) icing
    (confectioners') sugar

Beat the egg yolks thoroughly with the fine sugar, citrus rind and liqueur. Whisk the egg whites stiffly, fold them quickly and thoroughly into the yolks and turn the mixture into a buttered and heated oval gratin dish. Make a crease down the middle of the mixture with a palette knife. Bake in a fairly hot oven for 15–18 minutes, then sprinkle with icing sugar and cook for a further minute or so. Serve immediately, for this omelette will deflate very quickly. For the liqueur, use any of the orange-flavoured ones or apricot or cherry brandy.

ORANGE SOUFFLÉ

6 servings:

2 oranges
4 tablespoons (5) curaçao
3 oz. (3 cups) sponge-cake
    crumbs
½ pint (1¼ cups) milk
1 oz. (2 tablespoons) butter

3 oz. (full ⅓ cup) fine sugar
2½ oz. (scant ⅔ cup) plain
    flour
4 egg yolks
5 egg whites, stiffly whisked
icing (confectioners') sugar

Peel one orange and cut the rind into thin (julienne) strips. Blanch the strips in boiling water until soft. Drain them and marinate them in 1 tablespoon (1¼) curaçao. Peel the oranges and remove the segments by cutting each one close to the dividing membranes. Soak the crumbs in 3 tablespoons (3¾) curaçao and add the orange segments. Butter a 7½-in., 3-pint (2-quart) soufflé dish. Reserve 6 tablespoons (7½) of the milk and put the rest in a saucepan with the butter and sugar. Bring the mixture to the boil. Blend the reserved milk with the flour to a smooth paste. Whisk the paste into the milk and bring it quickly back to the boil. Continue stirring until the mixture thickens and leaves the sides of the pan (this is the panada). Off the heat, beat the yolks, one by one, into the panada. Stir in the curaçao from the marinated peel. Fold the egg whites into the panada and pour half of it into the soufflé dish. Spoon in the orange segments and crumbs. Pour the remaining soufflé mixture over them. Bake at 400°F., mark 6, for about 45 minutes. Remove from oven, sprinkle with icing sugar and julienne strips and serve immediately.

43

STRAWBERRY SOUFFLÉ

Steep 6 oz. (1½ cups) freshly sliced strawberries in 2 tablespoons (2½) orange juice, 2 tablespoons (2½) curaçao and fine sugar to taste. Drain the strawberries, retaining the juice. Line the base of a buttered soufflé dish with strawberries. Make up the basic soufflé recipe using vanilla-flavoured milk, and proceed as for the basic soufflé. While it is cooking whip the marinade into whipped cream to serve separately.

pies, tarts and flans

When the pie was opened the birds began to sing – quite literally. The trick
was that the four-and-twenty blackbirds weren't really baked in the pie but
put in just before it was served. The sixteenth-century Italian recipe, in a
cookbook translated into English in 1598, provided for a big lidded pie to be
baked 'blind', filled with flour. Through a hole cut in the base the flour was
taken out and at the last moment the birds and then a smaller real pie were
inserted. The birds flew out when the large pie was opened and the guests
had the real pie as consolation lest they should feel mocked. Similarly a 1660
recipe concealed live frogs in a pie designed, on the frogs' escape at table, to
'cause the ladies to squeak and hop about'.

Some of the recipes in this chapter have just as ancient a lineage but are
not quite as startling. They use mainly simple rubbed-in shortcrust and flan
(or biscuit crust) pastry. Rough puff is here too as a handy alternative for
homely pie toppings. More specialized pastries are in chapter 10.

PASTRY-MAKING

The golden rule for making these pastries is: play it cool. Keep hands, uten-
sils, working surfaces and ingredients as cool as possible. Even the small
amounts of water or other liquids for mixing are better iced, and a cold
marble slab is ideal for rolling out. Play it cool with the dough too – don't
fuss it. Handle it as little as you can and only with the finger tips. And play
it cool when flouring the rolling pin and the board – the minimum of flour,
so that you don't alter the balance of your carefully weighed ingredients and
so affect the texture of your pastry. All pastry benefits from a rest between
mixing and rolling and it is better to rest it in the refrigerator. Rubbed-in
and rough puff dough can be stored (in a plastic bag) in the refrigerator for

some days; but when you take dough from a very cold refrigerator let it stand a little while at room temperature before rolling it.

Keeping everything cool means that the fats and the tiny air pockets in the the dough give maximum expansion in the oven and make for lighter pastry. It is to increase the aeration that you always sift the flour and salt into the mixing bowl and you lift the flour from the bowl with the fingertips, while rubbing in, for the same reason. Add liquids with extreme care, for a sticky dough will mean tired and tough pastry. Temperature is important, again, in the cooking, so pre-heat the oven to the correct level before the pie or tart goes in.

Ingredients
Plain flour is best for shortcrust and flaked pastry. Combinations of butter with lard and other fats are often used in plain shortcrust pastry but use butter alone for flavour and texture in richer doughs.

Rolling out
Roll lightly but firmly with equal pressure from both hands and only in one direction (away from you), lifting the rolling pin at the end of each stroke. Preferably roll short pastry only once. Roll pastry for lining a dish about 2 in. larger than the flan tin or pie dish and, for a lid, at least ½ in. larger in diameter than the dish. Make proportionate allowances for patty tins and other individual pies and tartlets. To avoid stretching rolled-out dough, lift it on the rolling pin.

Assembling
Line the dish or tin by pressing the dough well into place and, for open pies and tarts, flute the edges by pressing with fork or fingertips. Trim off round the dish with a knife. After filling a two-crust pie moisten the edges of the lining and press on the edges of the top crust to seal it well. Make a slit or slits in the top for steam to escape and glaze the top with brushed-on milk or beaten egg yolk. For topping a single-crust pie, cut strips of pastry about 1 in. wide. Moisten the rim of the filled dish and press strips of pastry on it all round. Moisten this rim pastry, lift on the lid, press the edges and trim them.

Baking 'blind'
This is simply baking empty pastry cases for filling and possibly further cooking later. Line the pie tin with pastry and prick the base with a fork. Cut a buttered greaseproof paper slightly larger than the base of the tin and fit it, buttered side down, on to the pastry. Half-fill the tin with uncooked haricot (dried) beans. Bake it in a hot oven for about 15 minutes – long enough to set

46

the crust without browning it. Remove the beans and paper and let the case cool. Fill it with the chosen filling and bake in a moderate oven until the pie is done (see individual recipes). Blind-baked cases can be stored but after the initial cooking, as above. Return them to the oven under moderate heat for a further 10–15 minutes to brown and finish cooking. Let them cool on a wire rack before storing them in airtight tins.

BASIC SHORTCRUST PASTRY

This basic recipe makes enough for a 1½–2-pint (1-quart) pie dish for a single-crust pie or for a double-crust pie baked in an 8-in. dish.

8 oz. (2 cups) plain flour **4 oz. (½ cup) butter**
½ teaspoon (⅔) salt **cold water to mix**

Sieve together the flour and salt. Cut the butter into small flakes and, using the fingertips, lightly rub it into the flour until the mixture resembles fine fresh breadcrumbs. (If you are hot-handed mix the flaked butter into the flour with a knife.) Add cold water a little at a time, sprinkling it over the flour and mixing it with a knife. The mixture should bind together in one lump, leaving the sides of the bowl clean. Turn it out on to a lightly-floured board and leave it to rest in a cold place for about 15 minutes. Roll out, preferably only once, handling as little as possible. Use it as required.

FLAN PASTRY

This richer mix, enough for a 9-in. flan case, can be used as an alternative to the basic shortcrust in my recipes.

6 oz. (1½ cups) plain flour **1 teaspoon (1¼) lemon juice**
½ teaspoonful salt **2 oz. (¼ cup) fine sugar**
4 oz. (½ cup) butter **1 egg, beaten**

Sift the flour and salt into a mixing bowl. Add the butter in small flakes, rubbing it in lightly with the fingertips. Combine the lemon juice, sugar and egg and stir them in with a knife until all the ingredients begin to amalgamate. While the dough is still stiff and dry gather it into a ball, wrap it in plastic and put it in the refrigerator for at least an hour. Roll it, on a lightly floured board, to about ⅛-in. thickness.

47

ROUGH PUFF PASTRY

Rough puff is a quick and simple way of making a rich flaked pastry – fine for fruit-pie lids and mincemeat pies, for instance.

8 oz. (2 cups) plain flour
½ teaspoon (⅔) salt
6 oz. (¾ cup) butter

1 teaspoon (1¼) lemon juice
cold water to mix

Sieve together the flour and salt. Cut the butter into 1-in. cubes and drop them into the flour, stirring lightly until the butter is coated. Add the lemon juice gradually and sufficient water to make a soft but not sticky dough. On a lightly floured board or marble surface roll it into an oblong about ¼ in. thick. Fold it, bringing the top third over the centre and then folding the bottom third over it and put in it a cold place for ½ hour. Roll it out again and fold again. Giving the pastry a half-turn each time, repeat the rolling and folding 3–4 times. Leave it for an hour in a very cold place and then roll it out to ⅛ in. thickness. Bake desserts in small cases in a very hot oven for 10–20 minutes. When the pastry is a pie covering, cook the pie in a very hot oven for about 15 minutes to let the pastry rise, reduce heat to moderate and cook for 30–40 minutes more.

APPLE PIE

'Your breathe is like the steame of apple pyes' was a compliment written to a lady in the days of Queen Elizabeth I. These fragrant pies were, we know from the number of recipes that survive, very popular then and, of all the traditional English pies, are still the great favourite.

4–6 servings:
1½ lb. cooking apples
4 oz. (½ cup) sugar
4 cloves (or pinch of powdered cinnamon)

grated zest of ½ lemon
1–2 tablespoons (1¼–2½) water
1 basic shortcrust recipe

Preheat the oven to hot. Peel, core and quarter the apples and slice them, not too thinly. Layer them in the pie dish with the sugar, spice and lemon zest. Sprinkle with water. Roll out the pastry ¼ in. thick. Cut strips of pastry wide enough to cover the rim, dampen them and press them on the rim all round. Moisten the strip, lift on the pastry lid and press the edges firmly together. Trim, shape the edges, make a slit in the top of the pie and, if you like, decorate it with pastry trimmings. Bake for 15–20 minutes towards the top of the oven until the pastry is lightly browned, then reduce temperature

Plum Pudding (page 24)
and Pineapple Upside-down Pudding (page 37)

to moderate and bake until the fruit is cooked, about 20 minutes more. Dredge with sugar before serving hot with clotted cream.

DEEP FRUIT PIES

The apple pie above is called a deep fruit pie. Use the same method with almost any fruit or with young pink rhubarb. For other variations mix apples or other fruit with raspberries, loganberries or blackberries in season.

DOUBLE-CRUST FRUIT PIES

Blackcurrants and redcurrants and blueberries (bilberries or in Scotland blaeberries) are specially delicious for these 'plate' pies though, again, any fruits can be used.

4–6 servings:
1½ lb. blackcurrants   **1 basic shortcrust recipe**
4 oz. (½ cup) sugar   **milk to glaze**
1 tablespoon (1¼) flour

Hull and wash the fruit and mix it with the sugar and flour. Roll out half the pastry thinly (about ⅛-in. thick) and line an 8-in. pie plate. Put the fruit mixture on it. Roll out the remaining pastry, damp the edges of the pastry on the dish and cover the fruit with the lid. Press the edges well together with a fork or crimp them with the fingers and brush the top with milk. Cook in a preheated moderately hot oven until the crust is golden and the fruit is tender, about 30 minutes.

CHERRY PIE (*Illustrated*)

Following the blackcurrant pie recipe (above), substitute 1 lb. stoned cherries for the blackcurrants.

TREACLE TART (*Illustrated*)

4 servings:
1 flan pastry recipe (page 47)   **4 oz. (3⅔ cups) fresh white**
12 tablespoons (¾ cup)   **breadcrumbs**
   golden syrup   **coarsely grated rind 1 lemon**
2 oz. (¼ cup) butter

Roll out the pastry and line an 8-in. flan tin. Flute the edges. Warm the syrup and butter gently in a pan, add the breadcrumbs and lemon rind and spread the mixture in the pastry case. Cook towards the top of a hot oven for about 20 minutes. Serve hot or cold, with or without cream.

TOP *Creamy Syllabub (page 73) and Frothy Syllabub (page 74)*   51
BOTTOM *Treacle Tart (page 51) and Cherry Pie (page 51)*

JAM TARTS

Open jam tarts are cooked in the same way as the treacle tart above, either on a pie plate, in which case the edges of the pastry are fluted, or in a flan tin. Do not overfill the pastry case or the jam may boil and overflow during cooking.

PINEAPPLE PIE

This is a Jamaican recipe.

6 servings:

1 basic shortcrust recipe (page 47)
1 lb. fresh pineapple flesh
8 oz. (1 cup) sugar
1 oz. (¼ cup) plain flour

½ teaspoon (⅔) grated nutmeg
1 teaspoon (1¼) ground cinnamon
pinch salt
1½ oz. (3 tablespoons) butter

With two-thirds of the pastry, line a pie plate, prick the base and chill until needed. Cut the pineapple into small chips. Combine it with the sugar, flour, spices and salt and cook over low heat until the mixture thickens. Beat in the butter and let the mixture cool. Pour it into the pie shell. With the rest of the pastry make strips ¼ in. wide and arrange over the filling in lattice or radial design. Moisten the pie's rim and press a pastry strip firmly on to it all round, covering the ends of the criss-cross pieces. Bake it in a hot oven for 10 minutes. Then reduce the heat to moderate for about 30 minutes more.

PUMPKIN PIE

Although the English enjoyed pompions or pumpkins as early as Tudor times, the Americans have made pumpkin pie particularly their own. It is their traditional Thanksgiving pie. In Britain as in the United States pumpkins are all members of the Cucurbita family which takes in also some things Americans call squashes (butternut squash, for example, and table queen or acorn squash). The Americans have developed many varieties. They can have sweet cheese pumpkin and other evocative names are Kentucky field pumpkin, Japanese pie, green-striped and golden Cushaw, Canadian and winter crookneck, large yellow or Connecticut field, winter luxury, sugar or New England pie pumpkin.

4–6 servings:

1 lb. pumpkin flesh
1 flan pastry recipe
2 eggs, beaten
4 oz. (½ cup) fine sugar

4 tablespoons (5) milk
pinch grated nutmeg
pinch ground ginger
2 teaspoons (2½) ground cinnamon

Cut the pumpkin flesh into pieces and steam it until tender, 15–20 minutes. Mash it well or put it through a blender. Roll out the pastry thinly and line an 8-in. flan case. Trim and flute the edges. Beat the eggs with the sugar and beat in the pumpkin, milk and spices. Blend thoroughly and pour into the pastry case. Bake in the centre of a hot oven for 15 minutes, reduce the heat to moderate and cook until the filling is set, about 30 minutes more. Serve warm with cream.

LEMON MERINGUE PIE

Americans have made lemon meringue pie such a favourite that many believe it was born in the United States. It has long been enjoyed in many countries, however, and though simple to make, it deservedly ranks as one of the great dishes of the world. The recipe here is the one most popular in Britain. There are, of course, variations.

4 servings:

½ **basic shortcrust recipe** (page 47)	**3 oz. (full ⅓ cup) sugar**
1 oz. (2 tablespoons) cornflour (cornstarch)	**½ oz. (1 tablespoon) butter**
	2 egg yolks
½ **pint (1¼ cups) milk**	for the meringue:
1 lemon	**2 egg whites**
	4 oz. (½ cup) fine sugar

Roll out the pastry ⅛-in. thick, line a 7-in. flan case, flute the edges and bake blind in a hot oven for about 15 minutes. Leave to cool. Blend the cornflour with a little of the milk. Heat the rest of the milk with the grated lemon rind and pour it on to the blended cornflour. Return it to the pan and boil it gently for 2–3 minutes, stirring all the time. Remove it from the heat and stir in the sugar, butter and then the beaten egg yolks. Add the juice of the lemon and turn the mixture into the pastry case. Cook in a moderate oven for about 20 minutes. Meantime whisk the egg whites until they are stiff, add 2 oz. (¼ cup) fine sugar and whisk stiff again. Fold in nearly all the remaining sugar and spoon the meringue on to the lemon mixture, swirling it for finish and dredging with the remaining sugar. Put it back to cook in a slow oven until the meringue is crisp and lightly coloured, about 25–30 minutes more. Serve warm or cold.

LEMON (SOUFFLÉ) PIE

A further variation on the theme that's quite delicious is called either lemon pie or lemon soufflé pie. Ingredients are roughly the same as for lemon meringue pie though the cornflour is omitted. A lemon or orange chiffon pie can be made by piling the chiffon (see page 77) into a cold biscuit flan case or a pastry case.

6 servings:

1 flan pastry recipe (page 47)	**4 tablespoons (5) lemon juice**
4 egg yolks	**1 teaspoon (1¼) grated lemon**
6 oz. (¾ cup) sugar	**rind**
½ teaspoon (⅔) ground nutmeg	**4 egg whites**
or mace	**fine sugar**

Roll out the pastry thinly to line a 9-in. flan case and bake it blind in a hot oven for about 15 minutes. Leave it to cool. Whisk well the egg yolks and add 2 oz. (¼ cup) of the sugar, the spice and the lemon juice. Cook the mixture in a bowl over hot water, stirring constantly until the mixture thickens. Remove from the heat and mix in the grated lemon rind. In a clean bowl whisk the egg whites until they froth, gradually adding the remainder of the sugar, and beat until stiff. Fold them gently and gradually into the warm lemon mixture. Spoon the mixture into the baked pastry case, swirling it into peaks. Bake in the centre of a warm oven (325°F., mark 3) until the filling is golden and set. Cool a little before serving. Serve with a dusting of fine sugar.

CUSTARD TART

Since the Middle Ages custards in pastry cases – coffins as they were called then – have been popular and many variations have developed. One is to line the base of the case with black cherry jam or some stoned fresh cherries previously soaked in cherry brandy or kirsch. Another adds the grated rind of ½ lemon or orange to the custard mixture. The Brazilians put 1 cup (1¼) of grated coconut into the custard and call it coconut pie.

6–8 servings:

1 basic shortcrust or flan	**¾ pint (scant 2 cups) milk**
pastry recipe (page 47)	**vanilla pod**
2 whole eggs (or 3 yolks)	**1½ oz. (3 tablespoons) butter**
1 oz. (2 tablespoons) sugar	**nutmeg**

Line a shallow fireproof dish with pastry and flute the edges. Bake blind in a hot oven for 10 minutes and allow to cool. Meanwhile beat the eggs lightly with the sugar. Heat the milk, flavoured with a piece of vanilla pod, but do not boil it. Pour it gradually on to the eggs, stirring constantly. Stir in a walnut of butter and strain the custard into the pastry case. Dot it with butter and grate some nutmeg over it. Bake in the middle of a moderate oven until the custard sets, about 40 minutes. Serve cooled but not chilled.

BAKED BANANA PIE

6–8 servings:

1 basic shortcrust recipe	**4 oz. ($\frac{1}{2}$ cup) sugar**
6–8 ripe bananas	**1 teaspoon (1$\frac{1}{4}$) grated nutmeg**
$\frac{1}{2}$ pint (1$\frac{1}{4}$ cups) orange juice	**$\frac{1}{2}$ oz. (1 tablespoon)**
2 teaspoons (2$\frac{1}{2}$) lime or	**arrowroot**
lemon juice	**1 oz. (2 tablespoons) butter**

Line a pie dish with the pastry, prick the base, bake blind and let it cool. Put the peeled bananas in a well-greased baking tin. Mix the citrus juices, sugar and nutmeg well and pour them over the bananas. Bake in a moderate oven until the bananas soften, about 30 minutes. Remove the bananas carefully and let them cool. Mix the arrowroot with a little cold water, thicken the syrup with it and beat in the butter. Arrange the bananas in the pie shell, pour the syrup over them and, when cool, serve topped with chilled coconut cream (page 156).

TURNOVERS

Turnovers are a good way of using surplus dough. The usual fillings are jam, mincemeat (page 57) and fruit, chopped or puréed. Cut the thinly-rolled ($\frac{1}{8}$ in.) dough in squares or circles, brush the top side with water and put the filling on one half, to within $\frac{1}{2}$ in. of the edge. Fold the other half over and press the edges well together. Brush with beaten egg white, prick the top with a fork, sprinkle with sugar and bake in a preheated hot oven until golden, about 15 minutes. In Latin America they are deep-fried in very hot oil and served with flavoured sugar syrup.

CRUMBLE TOPS

A rubbed in cake mixture makes a good topping over fruit instead of pastry. Use 3 oz. ($\frac{3}{4}$ cup) sifted plain flour, 1$\frac{1}{2}$ oz. (3 tablespoons) flaked butter and 3 oz. (full $\frac{1}{3}$ cup) sugar (fine or brown) and work together with the fingertips until they are like breadcrumbs. Strew the crumble over the fruit in the pie dish and bake in a fairly hot oven until crisp and golden, 20–30 minutes. Optionally incorporate a pinch of ground cinnamon or grated rind of an orange or lemon with the mixture. Note that with this cooking time you may want to pre-cook some types of fruit a little if you like your fruits well done.

SPONGE FLAN CASES

The bases of many pleasant cold sweets, sponge flan cases can conveniently be made a day or two in advance and stored in airtight tins. For a flan tin 8½ in. × 1 in. use 2 eggs, 2 oz. (¼ cup) fine sugar and 2 oz. (½ cup) plain flour. Butter the flan tin, whisk the eggs and sugar together until thick and pale and the mixture leaves a trail when the whisk is lifted. Fold in the flour lightly with a metal spoon and turn the mixture into the flan tin. Preheat the oven to hot and bake until the sponge is well risen and firm to the touch, 10–15 minutes. Loosen the edge carefully and turn the case out on to a wire rack to cool. Fillings for sponge flans are given in chapter 9.

BISCUIT (COOKIE or CRACKER) AND CEREAL FLAN CASES

These uncooked cases give a deliciously crisp and contrasting texture to creamy fillings (see chapter 6). The following mixtures are sufficient for a pie plate or sandwich tin of 7–8 in.

BISCUIT (COOKIE CRUMB) CRUST

Crush 6 oz. (1½ cups) wholemeal or wheatmeal biscuits or gingernuts with a rolling pin, mix them with 1 tablespoon (1¼) of fine sugar and blend with 3 oz. (full ⅓ cup) melted butter. Butter the dish and line it with the mixture, pressing firmly into place. Chill until set. For variation – in harmony with the filling you choose – replace 1 oz. (¼ cup) of the biscuit crumb with 1 oz. (about ⅓ cup) chopped nuts or shredded coconut. Or add the grated rind of 1 lemon. Or add 1–2 teaspoons (1¼–2½) ground ginger or mixed spice. Or omit the sugar and bind the crumbs with 3–4 oz. (3–4 squares) grated chocolate melted with the butter.

CORNFLAKE CRUST

Crush 3 oz. (2¼ cups) cornflakes roughly by hand. Heat together in a pan 2 oz. (¼ cup) butter, 2 oz. (¼ cup) sugar and 1 tablespoon (1¼) golden syrup until melted and bubbly. Pour this over the cornflakes in a bowl and stir. Line the greased tin or dish with the mixture, pressing firmly. Chill until set.

MERINGUE FLAN CASES

Since they can be made in advance and stored for several days in an airtight tin, meringue cases have practical advantages. An 8-in. case requires

56

3 egg whites and 6 oz. ($\frac{3}{4}$ cup) fine sugar. Whisk the whites until stiff and then whisk in half the sugar until stiff again. Fold in the remaining sugar. Draw an 8-in. circle on a piece of silicone paper and put the paper on a baking sheet. Spread some of the meringue over the circle to form the flan base and build the walls by piping meringue around the edges. Bake in the coolest part of the slowest oven until dry, about $1\frac{1}{2}$ hours. Cool on a wire rack before removing the paper. If you fill your flan cases with fruit or any moist filling, line the inside first with cream to prevent the juices softening the meringue.

MINCEMEAT

Traditional mincemeat belongs particularly to Christmas and they say you'll have twelve lucky months if you eat a dozen pies or tarts between Christmas and New Year. But mincemeat is also a splendid store-cupboard companion – for fritters, won tons and other desserts; so it is worth making plenty. With the recipe below it will keep a year or more. These ingredients make 6 lb. mincemeat, probably most conveniently stored in 1-lb. jars.

$\frac{3}{4}$ **lb. (2 cups) seedless raisins**
$\frac{1}{4}$ **lb. (1 cup) chopped candied peel**
$\frac{3}{4}$ **lb. (2 cups) currants**
$\frac{1}{2}$ **lb. (1$\frac{1}{3}$ cups) sultanas (white raisins)**
1 lb. (3 cups) demerara sugar
1 lb. (4 cups) shredded suet
grated peel of 1 each orange and lemon

juice of 1 each orange and lemon
1 teaspoon (1$\frac{1}{4}$) grated nutmeg
$\frac{1}{2}$ **teaspoon ($\frac{2}{3}$) ground ginger**
$\frac{1}{4}$ **teaspoon ($\frac{1}{3}$) ground mace**
$\frac{1}{4}$ **teaspoon ($\frac{1}{3}$) ground cloves**
2–3 medium apples, peeled, cored and diced
$\frac{1}{2}$ **pint (1$\frac{1}{4}$ cups) brandy**

Chop the raisins and mix them in a large bowl with the candied peel, currants, sultanas, sugar, suet, citrus peels, citrus juices and spices. Add the apples and sufficient brandy to make the whole mixture moist but not runny. Pot the mixture in cold sterilized jam jars, pressing down well to expel air bubbles. Fill each jar quite full; cover it with waxed paper and a tight-fitting lid. Store the jars in a cool dark dry place.

MINCE PIES

With shortcrust or rough puff pastry based on 1 lb. flour, 1 lb. mincemeat is enough for about 24 mince pies in 2$\frac{1}{2}$-in. patty tins. Make a small slit in the top of each pie, brush them with milk and bake towards the top of a hot oven (425°F., mark 7) until golden brown, 15–20 minutes. When serving them hot from the oven one may lift the lids and slip in a spoonful of thick clotted cream or whipped cream on to the mincemeat.

ROYAL MINCE PIES

Eliza Acton in her 1845 recipe calls these pies 'iced' because of their meringue topping. The less confusing 'royal' title comes from Sheila Hutchins. Since her recipe dates from the early nineteenth century she speculates that they may have been enjoyed by the Prince Regent and his lady, Mrs Fitzherbert, in their times of dalliance at Brighton. This recipe makes 12 patties.

1 flan pastry recipe (page 47)	**juice of 1 lemon**
$\frac{1}{2}$ **oz. (1 tablespoon) butter**	**4 oz. ($\frac{1}{4}$ cup) mincemeat**
1 oz. (2 tablespoons) sugar	for the topping:
2 egg yolks	**2 egg whites**
1 lemon rind	**4 oz. ($\frac{1}{2}$ cup) fine sugar**

Preheat the oven to moderate. Thinly roll the pastry and line patty tins with it. Melt the butter and mix it with the sugar, beaten yolks, grated rind, lemon juice and mincemeat. Fill the patties three-quarters full and bake, uncovered, about 30 minutes. For the topping whisk the egg whites until very stiff, fold in the fine sugar and whisk again until stiff. Remove the patties from oven and reduce the heat to slow. Cover each patty with meringue mixture and return them to the oven until lightly browned, about 30 minutes.

MINCEMEAT TART

For people who love plenty of mincemeat without too much pastry, make an open tart. Line an 8-in. flan tin with flan pastry (page 47) and trim the edges. Fill the case almost to the top with mincemeat. Roll out the pastry trimmings and cut $\frac{1}{4}$-in. strips to criss-cross the mincemeat. Bake the tart just above the centre of a fairly hot oven (375°F., mark 5) for about 30 minutes. Serve it hot with cream or vanilla ice cream. It may be served cold as well.

For variation line the uncooked pastry case with 2 peeled, cored and sliced cooking apples, sprinkled with lemon juice before putting in the mincemeat.

milk puddings and custards

Puddings 'like Mother used to make' are enduringly popular. Perhaps it is nostalgia for the uncomplicated things of childhood. More probably, I like to think, it is the appeal of their cooking, simple but good. At any rate, there they are – regulars alike in home eating and in the menus of top hotels and restaurants. Milk puddings, one of the most popular of all sweet puddings, in this context embrace hot and cold sweets made with milk and grain or flour (rice, tapioca, sago, semolina) as well as milk jellies, junkets and custards. In the recipes containing rice the short-grain (Carolina) rice is used.

BASIC BAKED RICE PUDDING

4 servings:

1½ oz. (¼ cup) rice   1 pint (2½ cups) rich milk
1 oz. (2 tablespoons) butter   grated nutmeg or ground
1 oz. (2 tablespoons) sugar   cinnamon
pinch of salt

Wash the rice and put it into a well-buttered 2-pint (1½-quart) oven-proof dish with the sugar and salt. Add the milk, sprinkle it with spice and dot it with shavings of butter. Bake it toward the bottom of a slow oven (300°F., mark 2) for 2½ hours, stirring it once or twice in the first half-hour. The slower and longer you cook the pudding, the creamier it will be.
Variations: 2 oz. (⅓ cup) sultanas and/or a little grated lemon or orange zest can be added at the initial stage.

When I was a child my mother sometimes cooked rice, with the appropriate amount of milk and water, in a double saucepan, with raisins and sultanas and a grating of nutmeg or allspice. Then she would add hot custard sauce to it. I remember it well rather more for the fact that I played somewhat fiercer hockey afterwards than for the detailed recipe. The Italians like a variation on the theme – especially the Sicilians, so perhaps there's a parallel. Anyway, Ada Boni's *dolce di castagne e riso* in her *Italian Regional Cooking* inspired that remembrance in me once again. That Italian name for this rice pudding with a difference translates as:

CHESTNUT AND RICE PUDDING (*Illustrated*)

6 servings:

5 oz. (1 full cup) dried chestnuts
2 pints (5 cups) milk or water
pinch salt

10 oz. (1⅔ cups) rice
3½ oz. (scant ½ cup) sugar
2½ oz. (full ⅓ cup) sultanas
2 oz. (¼ cup) butter

Put the chestnuts in warm water and leave them overnight. Drain them and put them into a pan with the milk to cover and a pinch of salt. Bring them slowly to the boil, reduce heat, cover and cook for about 30 minutes. Add the rice and continue cooking until it is *al dente*, the grains still separate, adding more milk as necessary. Just before it is cooked, add the sugar and sultanas, melt the butter and stir it gently. Cool it before serving. Or coat a bowl with butter and sugar, pack the pudding in and chill it thoroughly in the refrigerator so that it can be turned out as a mould. There is no need for garnish or sauce, although single cream is good poured over it and also combines well with sharper soft fruits such as loganberries or raspberries.

RICH RICE PUDDING

4–6 servings:

2 oz. (⅓ cup) rice
¼ pint (full ½ cup) water
1½ pints (3¾ cups) milk
grated rind ½ lemon

¼ pint (full ½ cup) double (heavy) cream
1 oz. (2 tablespoons) sugar
2 eggs, separated
butter

Wash the rice and cook it gently in an uncovered heavy-based pan until the water is absorbed. Add the milk and lemon rind and simmer slowly until the rice is soft, stirring occasionally. Remove the pan from the heat and when the contents cool stir in the cream, sugar and beaten egg yolks. Whisk the egg whites stiffly, fold them into the mixture and pour it into a buttered 2-pint (1½-quart) pie dish. Bake it in the centre of a moderate oven until it is risen and golden, about 30 minutes.

CREAMED RICE

4 servings:

1½ oz. (¼ cup) rice
1 pint (2½ cups) milk
1 oz. (2 tablespoons) sugar

¼ pint (full ½ cup) double
(heavy) cream, whipped

Wash the rice and put it with the milk and sugar into the top of a double saucepan. Cook for 1½–2 hours until creamy, removing the lid after the first half-hour. Stir it occasionally. Allow it to cool slightly before stirring in the whipped cream. Rice so prepared is a good basis for both hot and cold desserts served with fruits and fruit sauces (chapter 9).

RICE MOULD

Using the creamed rice method, increase the rice to 2 oz. (⅓ cup). When it is almost cold pack it into a wet mould. Turn it out when set and decorate it with glacé or crystallized fruits or serve with fruit, jam sauce (page 33) or zabaglione sauce (page 74).

EMPRESS RICE (*Riz à l'impératrice*)

Prepare the creamed rice recipe and when it is fairly cool, fold in 2 oz. (⅓ cup) chopped crystallized fruits soaked in kirsch. Stir in ½ pint (1¼ cups) thick custard sauce (page 66) and set in a mould. Peaches (or other fruits) *à l'impératrice* are poached and glazed fruits adorning rice *à l'impératrice*.

SPICED SEMOLINA

4 servings:

1 pint (2½ cups) milk
1½ oz. (3 tablespoons) semolina
3 oz. (full ⅓ cup) sugar
1–2 teaspoons (1¼–2½) mixed spice

grated rind ½ lemon
2 oz. (⅓ cup) sultanas
2 eggs, separated

Heat the milk in a saucepan, sprinkle on the semolina, bring to the boil and cook for a few minutes, stirring constantly. Beat the egg yolks. Remove the pan from the heat, stir in half the sugar, the spice, lemon rind, sultanas and beaten egg yolks. Pour the mixture into a buttered pie dish. Whisk the egg whites stiffly, fold in the remaining sugar and pile on top of the pudding. Bake towards the top of a fairly hot oven (400°F., mark 6) until the meringue is lightly browned, about 10 minutes. Alternatively, whisk in the egg whites as for rich rice pudding (page 60) and bake in the centre of a moderate oven for about 30 minutes.

SPICED TAPIOCA AND SAGO

Tapioca can be cooked in the same way as spiced semolina. With sago, cook it for 5–10 minutes after bringing it to the boil.

BAKED TAPIOCA PUDDING

Pearl tapioca can be cooked in the same way as the basic baked rice or the rich rice pudding, substituting the same quantity of tapioca for the rice.

BANANA TAPIOCA

Some of the South Sea Islanders fry ripe bananas in butter, mash them well and mix them with an equal quantity of cooked sweetened tapioca and a little coconut cream (page 156). Then they set it in a mould and chill it. Whipped cream is just as good when coconut cream is not to hand.

BLANCMANGE AND CORNFLOUR (CORNSTARCH) MOULDS

In classic French cuisine blancmange was a jellied almond milk – from pounding almonds with water and sieving them. It is still sometimes made that way though the more popular modern version is 8 oz. (1⅓ cups) kirsch-flavoured ground almonds combined with 1 pint (2½ cups) Chantilly cream (page 139). The British blancmange is however a cornflour (cornstarch) mould. Similar moulds can be made with like quantities of ground rice.

BASIC CORNFLOUR (CORNSTARCH) MOULD

4 servings:
1 pint (2½ cups) flavoured milk   **2 oz. (¼ cup) sugar**
**1½ oz. (3 tablespoons) cornflour
  (cornstarch)**

Bring ¾ pint (scant 2 cups) of milk to the boil. Mix the cornflour and sugar to a smooth paste with the remaining cold milk. Strain the boiling milk over the paste, stirring, and return the mixture to the pan. Boil it for 5 minutes, pour it into a wet mould and let it cool. When cool, place it in the refrigerator to chill and set. Turn the pudding out of the mould before serving.

FLAVOURED CORNFLOUR (CORNSTARCH) MOULDS

Flavour the milk in the basic cornflour mixture (page 62) by infusing in it grated rind of ½ lemon or orange or a piece of vanilla pod. Serve the mould with a tangy fruit purée or with jam and cream. For variation cool the mixture and just before pouring it into the mould stir in 2 tablespoons (2½) of spirit or liqueur or a little almond or other essence.

For fruit moulds, pour half the mixture into the mould, spread jam or chopped fruit or nuts almost to the edge and then pour in the rest of the mixture.

For a chocolate mould, blend 1 tablespoon (1¼) cocoa with the cornflour, sugar and cold milk or dissolve 2 oz. (2 squares) bitter or plain chocolate in the boiling milk.

BAKED CORNFLOUR (CORNSTARCH) MOULD

For a richer pudding make the basic cornflour mould (page 62) mixture and cool it slightly. Beat into it 2 egg yolks, fold in 2 stiffly-whisked egg whites and bake it in a moderate oven for about 30 minutes.

BASIC WHITE SAUCE

The quantities in this recipe give ½ pint (1¼ cups) of sauce of pouring consistency. For a coating consistency use ¾ oz. (1½ tablespoons) butter and ¾ oz. (1½ tablespoons) cornflour (cornstarch). The sauce can be made in the same way with arrowroot. If lumps form, put the sauce through a sieve.

½ oz. (1 tablespoon) **cornflour**
  (**cornstarch**)
½ **pint (1¼ cups) milk**

1 oz. (2 tablespoons) sugar
½ oz. (1 tablespoon) butter

Blend the flour with a little of the milk and boil the rest with the sugar. Pour it over the blended flour, stirring continuously and return the mixture to the pan. Boil for 4 minutes and beat in the butter.

FLAVOURED CORNFLOUR (CORNSTARCH) SAUCES

Flavour basic white sauce (page 63) with spices, essences or 2 tablespoons (2½) spirit or liqueur. Or one may infuse a bay leaf and grated rind of 1 lemon or 1 orange in the milk and strain it.

For a richer sauce beat in 1 egg yolk when the sauce has cooled slightly.

For coffee sauce, substitute for the milk ½ pint (1¼ cups) very strong black coffee – about twice as strong as for drinking.

MILK JELLIES AND JUNKETS

Plain or mildly-flavoured milk jellies make a good foil to the sharper fruits and fruit sauces (chapter 9). For flavour variations in the jelly, omit the lemon rind and add a little almond or other essence.

MILK JELLY

4 servings:

2 oz. (¼ cup) fine sugar **1 pint (2½ cups) milk**
3 thin strips lemon rind **½ oz. (2 tablespoons) gelatine**

Put the sugar, lemon rind and milk in a saucepan over gentle heat and let it infuse for about 10 minutes. Bring it to boiling point and strain it on to the gelatine, stirring until the gelatine is dissolved. As the mixture cools stir it from time to time and when it is beginning to thicken pour it into a wet mould. Chill it and turn out when quite set.

HONEYCOMB MOULD

A light sweet that sets in two layers, the top having a fluffy honeycomb appearance from which it gets its name.

4 servings:

2 eggs, separated **½ oz. (2 tablespoons) gelatine**
1 pint (2½ cups) vanilla- **2 tablespoons (2½) water**
flavoured milk
1½ oz. (3 tablespoons) fine sugar

Make a custard (page 66) with the egg yolks, milk and sugar. Dissolve the gelatine in the water and add it to the cooled custard. Whisk the egg whites very stiffly and fold them into the custard. Pour it into a glass serving dish or mould it and turn it out when set. Serve it with chocolate sauce, coffee sauce or a purée of soft fruits.

ORANGE HONEYCOMB

Infuse a bay leaf in plain milk before making the custard (page 66) and proceed as above, adding the grated rind of 1 orange to the mixture with the gelatine. Turn it out when set and decorate with whipped cream and angelica.

BASIC JUNKET

Junket, the curds of curds and whey, is simply made by adding rennet to tepid milk. Rennet used in these recipes is the liquid kind sold without added flavouring or colour. Important factors to remember are to heat the milk only until it is just warm to the finger, not to chill it too rapidly and not to disturb it until it is served.

4 servings:

1 pint (2½ cups) milk

½–1 oz. (1–2 tablespoons) fine sugar
1 teaspoon (1¼) rennet

Warm the milk to blood heat, stirring in the sugar until it is dissolved. Remove it from the heat, stir in the rennet, pour the mixture at once into a serving dish or dishes and leave it at room temperature until set.

FLAVOURED JUNKETS

Grate nutmeg or chocolate over the junket (above) just before serving or serve cinnamon sugar or ground ginger on the side. Alternatively one may add 2 tablespoons (2½) rum or brandy or a little vanilla or other essence to the milk or dissolve 1½ oz. (1½ squares) chocolate in 3 tablespoons (3¾) of the milk and mix it in.

DEVONSHIRE JUNKET

Make the basic junket (above) and just before serving it cover the top with brandy-flavoured Devonshire (clotted) cream. Sprinkle it lightly with grated nutmeg or with mixed fine sugar and ground cinnamon. This dessert is so delightful as it is, I think the addition of vanilla or other flavouring to the milk spoils the subtlety.

CUSTARDS

Custards and custard sauces can be flavoured with essences or with spirits or liqueurs according to taste and occasion. Spice-flavoured milk and/or sugar (page 19) can make pleasant variations. Baked custard tart is on page 54.

BASIC CUSTARD

4 servings:

4 egg yolks
3 oz. (full $\frac{1}{3}$ cup) fine sugar

$\frac{1}{4}$ teaspoon ($\frac{1}{3}$) salt
1 pint ($2\frac{1}{2}$ cups) vanilla-flavoured milk

Beat the egg yolks with the sugar and salt until they are pale and fluffy. Heat the milk in a heavy-based pan but do not let it boil. Whisk a little of it into the egg mixture and then stir the mixture into the hot milk. Stir continuously over the gentlest heat – it must not boil – until it thickens.

CUSTARD SAUCE

Basic custard can be used hot or cold as a sauce. For thick custard sauce use only $\frac{3}{4}$ pint (scant 2 cups) flavoured milk.

BAKED CUSTARD

4 servings:

1 pint ($2\frac{1}{2}$ cups) milk
3 eggs

1 oz. (2 tablespoons) fine sugar
grated nutmeg

Warm the milk but do not let it boil. Whisk the eggs and sugar lightly in a bowl and pour the hot milk into it, stirring continuously. Strain the mixture into a buttered ovenproof dish and sprinkle it, if you wish, with grated nutmeg. Stand the dish in a baking tin containing a little cold water. (This tin precludes the custard from curdling or separating through overheating.) Bake in the centre of a warm oven (325°F., mark 3) until set, about 45 minutes.

DIPLOMAT PUDDING, HOT

A French favourite, cold diplomat pudding is in chapter 6 – quite a different recipe. The hot version, as prepared by Escoffier and other masters, is some-times cooked in a bain-marie or steamer instead of in the oven. Cooked in a

Chestnut and Rice Pudding (page 60)
and Caramel Custards (page 70)

mould (or individual moulds) it can be turned out and surrounded by syrup-poached fruits covered in their own thickened syrup.

6 servings:

18 sponge fingers	**2 whole eggs**
½ pint (1¼ cups) curaçao or rich rum	**4 egg yolks**
	2 oz. (¼ cup) fine sugar
3 oz. (¾ cup) mixed candied peel and fruits	**1 oz. (2 tablespoons) butter**
	for the garnish:
1 pint (2½ cups) milk	**½ pint (1¼ cups) fruit sauce**

Moisten the sponge finger biscuits – not so much as to make them sodden – in the curaçao or rum. Chop the candied peel and fruit and leave it to soak in the liquor. Heat the milk but do not let it boil. Whisk the whole eggs, egg yolks and sugar in a bowl and, still whisking all the time, gradually add the milk. Butter an ovenproof dish or mould and drain the chopped candied fruits. Arrange the biscuits in the dish, alternating a layer of biscuits with a layer of fruit. Slowly and carefully fill the dish with the egg-and-milk mixture. Stand the dish in a baking tin containing an inch or so of cold water. Bake in the centre of a warm oven (325°F., mark 3) until set, about 45 minutes. The fruit sauce is unnecessary if the garnish is poached fruit.

PINEAPPLE PUDDING

4 servings:

1 lb. ripe pineapple flesh	**2 eggs, separated**
3 tablespoons (3¾) kirsch	**1 oz. (¼ cup) flour**
5 oz. (scant ⅔ cup) fine sugar	**¾ pint (scant 2 cups) milk**
2 oz. (¼ cup) butter	

Shred the pineapple and let it marinate for an hour or so in the kirsch and 1 oz. (2 tablespoons) sugar. Cream the butter and 2 oz. (¼ cup) sugar until light and fluffy. Beat in the egg yolks and flour. Drain the pineapple and, if necessary, make the liquid up to ¼ pint (full ½ cup) with water. Warm this liquid with the milk but do not let it boil. Stirring all the time, gradually blend the milk with the butter-egg-flour mixture and when it is well blended return it to the pan to cook slowly until thick and creamy – but again without boiling. Spread the pineapple over the base of a 2½-pint (1½-quart) ovenproof dish and pour the custard mixture over it. Whisk the egg whites until stiff, add 1½ oz. (3 tablespoons) of sugar and whisk again. Spoon this meringue on top of the custard in four little rugged alps and sprinkle them with the remaining sugar. Bake at 300°F. (mark 1–2) till the meringue peaks are tinged with gold, about 30 minutes.

Coupe Jacques (page 98)
and Raspberry Spumoni (page 97)

69

CARAMEL CUSTARD (*Illustrated*)

Should you have the good fortune to go through the great sherry and brandy *bodegas* of Pedro Domecq in Jerez under the escort of the young and handsome José Domecq, he has the knowledge and the willingness to answer all your questions. That's how one learns that the finos and the amontillados are 'fined' (which is to say, cleared of things which might impair the clearness of the wine) with egg whites. It takes twenty egg whites to clear each butt. Since that leaves many egg yolks, the people in those parts make their caramel custard with yolks only and give it the name of *tocino de cielo* which roughly translates as heavenly bacon. It is quite delectable, though rather richer and more solid than the recipe here.

4 servings:

4 oz. (½ cup) sugar	**2 whole eggs**
2 tablespoons (2½) water	**2 egg yolks**
1 pint (2½ cups) milk	

Put 3 oz. (full ⅓ cup) of sugar with the water in a small pan. Dissolve the sugar slowly and then boil without stirring until you have a rich golden-brown syrup (310°F., 154°C.). Immediately pour this caramel into a warmed 6-in. cake tin or soufflé dish, turning the tin until the base and sides are well coated. Allow it to cool. Warm the milk, pour it on to the lightly whisked eggs and yolks, add the remaining sugar and strain the mixture over the cooled caramel. Stand the dish or tin in a shallow tin of water and bake just below the centre of a warm oven (325°F., mark 3) until set, 40–45 minutes. Let it stand a few minutes and then turn it on to a hot dish and serve at once. Or, to serve cold, leave it in the tin until completely cold before turning it out.

CARAMEL CREAM (*Crème brûlée*)

This caramel cream requires undivided attention in the making but the result is well worth the concentration. For a dinner party it is attractive when made in individual dishes. The cream can be made a day in advance and left in the refrigerator, but in this case the top of the cream should be dusted with sugar and caramelized only a couple of hours before serving. Put it back in the refrigerator after the caramelizing.

4 servings:

4 egg yolks	**1 pint (2½ cups) double**
4 oz. (½ cup) fine sugar	**(heavy) cream**
	vanilla essence

70

This pudding should be served in the same dish in which it is cooked. Beat the eggs with 3 oz. (full ⅓ cup) sugar until pale and frothy. Heat the cream gently without boiling it and pour it over the egg yolk mixture, stirring well. Return the mixture to the pan and cook on the gentlest heat to thicken it, but on no account let it boil. Stir in a little vanilla essence. Pour the mixture into the heatproof dish and leave it to cool. When it is cold, dust the surface with the remaining sugar so that it is evenly covered without being too thick. Brown it quickly under a pre-heated very hot grill. Remove it from the heat and chill it for 2–3 hours before serving. Since the caramel will be hard, tap it smartly with the back of a spoon to break it for easier serving at table.

CHOCOLATE CUSTARD CREAMS

6 servings:

8 oz. (8 squares) bitter chocolate
¾ pint (scant 2 cups) milk
4–5 oz. (full ½ cup) sugar

¼ pint (full ½ cup) double (heavy) cream
8 egg yolks

Break the chocolate and melt it gently in a thick pan; add the milk and bring it to the boil, stirring constantly. Thoroughly blend the sugar, cream and egg yolks in a bowl and then, stirring all the time, slowly add the boiling chocolate milk. Strain the mixture into 6 individual soufflé dishes or other oven-proof dishes. Stand them in a shallow pan of hot water and cook in the centre of a preheated warm oven (325°F., mark 3) for 25 minutes. Chill them before serving topped with whipped cream.

ENGLISH TRIFLE

Zuppa inglese is indeed a trifle but it is usually elaborated to such heights of fantasy that I am inclined to agree with Elizabeth David's description of it as 'that exuberant joke'. True English trifle, however, can be one of the most delicious of sweets and is quite simple to make. Its base used to be macaroons but is now, more often than not, sponge cake, preferably made the day before. This is the recipe I use most, though the variations are almost infinite. For instance, one may use a sweetened fruit purée instead of jam and almost any wine, spirit or syrup instead of sherry. Final decorative touches are a personal matter, though I think it a pity to make the top look like the decorations on a Christmas tree. Making trifles in one big bowl, as in the recipe here, is convenient for large parties but they look more elegant when made in individual glass dishes. The method is the same of course.

6–8 servings:

1 8-in. sponge cake

6 tablespoons (7½) medium-dry sherry

4 tablespoons (5) raspberry jam

2 oz. (¾ cup) ratafia biscuits, crushed

¾ pint (scant 2 cups) basic custard (page 66)

½ pint (1¼ cups) double (heavy) cream, whipped

1 oz. (scant ¼ cup) blanched almonds

Cut up the sponge cake and line a glass dish with it. Sprinkle it with 4 tablespoons sherry (or more, if preferred, to taste) and spread it with the jam. Cover with ratafias, sprinkle on more sherry and let it stand for half an hour. Make the custard and when it has slightly cooled pour it over the ratafias. Chill the trifle and just before serving it cover it with whipped cream and stick blanched almonds upright into the cream.

creams, whips and jellied sweets

Many of the most delectable creams, whips and jellies are easy to make and can be whipped up at a moment's notice or made in advance. One of my favourites is the syllabub.

SYLLABUBS

There are many variations on this old English recipe – including some which specify that the milk be milked straight from the cow into the bowl of sweetened spiced wine, ale, cider or whey. Here are two recipes using sherry or a sweetish white wine, which can be laced or even replaced with brandy. The first (creamy) syllabub can be made at least a day ahead without losing its shape or consistency.

CREAMY SYLLABUB (*Illustrated*)

4 servings:

1 lemon
$\frac{1}{4}$ pint (full $\frac{1}{2}$ cup) sherry or white wine

2 oz. ($\frac{1}{4}$ cup) sugar
$\frac{1}{2}$ pint (1$\frac{1}{4}$ cups) double (heavy) cream

Thinly pare the rind from the lemon. Squeeze the lemon and strain the juice. Mix the juice and rind with the wine and leave for several hours (or overnight). Strain it, add the sugar and gradually stir in the cream. Whisk until the mixture stands in peaks. Spoon it into 4 stemmed glasses, piling it above the rim of the glasses. Chill and serve, if you wish, with sponge (lady's) fingers or ice-cream wafers. Alternatively, you can crush 4 oz. (1 cup) ratafias, divide them into 4 individual bowls and spoon the syllabub over them.

FROTHY SYLLABUB (*Illustrated*)

4 servings:

2 egg whites	**¼ pint (full ½ cup) white wine**
4 oz. (½ cup) fine sugar	**½ pint (1¼ cups) double**
juice of ½ lemon	**(heavy) cream, whipped**

Whisk the egg whites stiffly and fold in the sugar, strained lemon juice, wine and whipped cream. Pour the mixture into individual glasses and chill for 2 hours before serving. When the mixture separates the top will be fluffy and the underneath clear, so you may both spoon and drink.

ZABAGLIONE

Zabaglione, also called *sabayon* (in France) and *zabaione*, can be made with sherry or any fortified wine.

4 servings:

8 egg yolks	**6 tablespoons (7½) marsala**
1½ oz. (3 tablespoons) sugar	

Beat the egg yolks with the sugar and marsala in a bowl until they are frothy. Put the bowl over a pan of hot (not boiling) water and whisk until the mixture thickens. Pour it into warmed glasses and serve immediately with macaroons or other biscuits.

ZABAGLIONE SAUCE

Served warm with almost anything from Christmas pudding to ice cream, *zabaglione* sauce is made in the same way as *zabaglione* but using 6 egg yolks, 2 oz. (¼ cup) sugar and 6–8 tablespoons (7½–10) marsala. You can stir in 2–3 tablespoons of brandy a few minutes after removing the sauce from the heat.

COLD MOUSSES

Mousse means froth or effervescence and the essence of dessert mousses is that they should be airy and light. Some mousses are also called cold soufflés and are set in a soufflé dish or individual soufflé dishes. Tie or tape a collar of double greaseproof paper around the dish projecting 2 in. above the rim to hold the piled-up mousse mixture until it sets. When it is set, cut the string or tape and ease the collar away with a warm knife. The following recipes

74

need a collared dish of 6-in. diameter and 1½-pint (2-quart) basic capacity. Frozen mousses, as distinct from those merely chilled, are in chapter 7.

FRUIT MOUSSE

4 servings:

4 eggs, separated
4 oz. (½ cup) fine sugar
½ pint (1¼ cups) fruit purée

½ oz. (2 tablespoons) gelatine, dissolved
½ pint (1¼ cups) double (heavy) cream

In a large bowl over hot (not boiling) water whisk the egg yolks and sugar until they are pale and frothy. Add the fruit purée and continue to whisk until the mixture begins to thicken. Cool it and add the gelatine. Meanwhile, lightly whip the cream, fold it through the fruit mixture and fold in the well-whisked egg whites. Turn it into a collared soufflé dish or dishes so that the mixture is about an inch above the rim. Leave it to set in the refrigerator. Remove the collar and decorate with cream and chopped nuts, whole berries or marshmallows.

CHERRY MOUSSE

Fruit mousses can also be made with whole or sliced fruits, such as berries, sliced bananas or cooking apples. For a cherry mousse, also called mousse Montmorency, bring 1 lb. stoned cherries to the boil in ½ pint (1¼ cups) of water with sugar to taste. Strain off the juice, let it cool and substitute it for the fruit purée in the recipe for fruit mousse (above). Decorate the top of the set mousse with the cooked cherries and a jam glaze.

CHOCOLATE MOUSSE

4 servings:

3 oz. (3 squares) bitter chocolate
4 eggs, separated

2 oz. (¼ cup) fine sugar

Melt the broken chocolate in a bowl over hot water. Beat the egg yolks with the sugar until pale and fluffy and add the melted chocolate. Stiffly whisk the egg whites and fold them into the chocolate mixture. (A mousse can be made lighter by folding in an extra whisked egg white.) Put the mixture into a serving dish or individual glasses and chill well in the refrigerator. This is a sweet that can be made a day or two ahead.

75

PRALINE MOUSSE

4 servings:

1 praline recipe (below)
3 eggs, separated
¼ pint (full ½ cup) milk
½ oz. (2 tablespoons)
  gelatine, dissolved
¼ pint (full ½ cup) double
  (heavy) cream

¼ pint (full ½ cup) single
  (light) cream
2 tablespoons (2½) coffee
  liqueur
2 oz. (⅓ cup) chopped toasted
  almonds

Make the praline. Beat the egg yolks and cook them gently with the milk in the top of a double saucepan until the mixture thickens. Cool it slightly and stir in the gelatine. Whip together the double and single creams and the liqueur and fold them into the egg yolk mixture just before it sets. Fold in the praline. Stiffly whisk the egg whites and fold them in. Pour into a collared soufflé dish and chill until set. Remove the collar and decorate the top and exposed sides with chopped almonds.

PRALINE FOR DESSERTS

Made in a larger quantity, sifted praline can be stored in air-tight tins or jars.

5 oz. (full ½ cup) sugar
2 tablespoons (2½) water

pinch of cream of tartar
2 oz. (⅓ cup) unblanched
  almonds

In a small saucepan dissolve the sugar in the water and add the cream of tartar and almonds. Boil until the syrup is golden brown (310°F., 154°C.) and pour it at once on to an oiled baking tray. When it is cold pound it finely or grind it finely in an electric blender and sift it. As variants to the almonds, use hazel nuts, walnuts or a mixture.

NUT SAUCE

Nut sauce can be made by combining 3 tablespoons (3¾) praline with ½ pint (1¼ cups) custard sauce (page 66) or white sauce (page 63). Optionally, also stir in 2 oz. (⅓ cup) toasted nuts, finely chopped.

FRUIT FOOLS

Almost any fruit purée (page 120) can be used in a fool though the sharpish flavour of gooseberry, rhubarb and blackberry add most to this dessert.

76

Blend ¾ pint (scant 2 cups) of sweetened fruit purée with ½ pint (1¼ cups) of double (heavy) cream or with ¼ pint (full ½ cup) of custard (page 66) and ¼ pint (full ½ cup) double (heavy) cream. Whisk the mixture or put it through an electric blender until it is thick and smooth. Spoon it into glasses and chill before serving, topped with chopped nuts and praline (page 76).

CHIFFONS AND CREAM WHIPS

Chiffons and whips are often similar to mousse mixtures. Indeed the mousse recipes can be used for whips, but as whips are served in glasses or used for filling flan cases of pastry, sponge, biscuit, cereal or meringue (chapter 4), they need only half as much gelatine or even none at all. They also make good centres for ring-moulded creamed rice, puréed chestnuts or jellies. Marshmallows cut into quarters and folded into chiffons and whips add textural variation. Fruit whips without cream or egg yolk are in chapter 9.

LEMON OR ORANGE CHIFFON

4 servings:

3 eggs, separated
3 oz. (full ⅓ cup) sugar

juice of 1 lemon
grated rind of ½ lemon

Beat together the egg yolks and sugar until pale and creamy, gradually add the strained lemon juice and the rind and stir over a pan of hot water until the mixture thickens. When it is cool, stiffly whisk the egg whites and fold them into the lemon mixture. Pile into individual glasses, chill and decorate, if you like, with sugar-frosted violets and mint leaves. As variants, use a Seville orange instead of a lemon or 3 tablespoons (3¾) of white wine and a little orange-flower water instead of juice.

STRAWBERRY CREAM WHIP

4 servings:

2 eggs, separated
2 oz. (¼ cup) sugar
½ pint (1¼ cups) double (heavy) cream, whipped

1 lb. strawberries, sliced

Whisk together the egg yolks and sugar until pale and foamy and then fold in the cream. Stiffly whisk the egg whites and fold them, with the strawberries, into the cream mixture. Turn into a serving dish or blind-baked flan case and chill.

BRANDY CREAM WHIP

4 servings:

½ pint (1¼ cups) double (heavy) cream	2 tablespoons (2½) brandy
4 egg yolks	1 tablespoon (1¼) curaçao
	sugar to taste

Whisk all the ingredients together in a bowl until the mixture is really thick. Pile it into a heatproof serving dish or individual dishes. Shake on sugar to cover the top evenly but not too thickly. Put under a very hot grill for a few seconds to brown. Chill in the refrigerator for a couple of hours and serve with fresh fruits or sponge fingers.

CHESTNUT CREAM WHIP

4 servings:

6 oz. (1 cup) sweetened chestnut purée	1½ oz. (¼ cup) marrons glacés
1 tablespoon (1¼) Tia Maria	½ pint (1¼ cups) double (heavy) cream, whipped
	2 egg whites

Mix the purée, liqueur and chopped marrons and fold them into the whipped cream. Fold in the stiffly whisked egg whites. Pile into individual glasses and chill. Serve them with ratafia biscuits.

MONT BLANC

4 servings:

1 lb. chestnuts	¼ pint (full ½ cup) double (heavy) cream, whipped
½ teaspoon (⅔) salt	
½ lb. (1 cup) sugar	2 tablespoons (2½) rum or brandy

Boil the chestnuts in water for 10 minutes. Shell and skin them and return them to a pan of cold water. Bring the water to the boil, then lower the heat and simmer until the chestnuts are tender, about 1 hour. Drain and mash them with the salt and sugar and put them through a ricer or a coarse sieve, letting them fall lightly into a high mound. Fold the rum or brandy into the cream and pile it over the chestnut mound in peaks.

CHESTNUT PUDDING

August Escoffier used to make what might be called a simpler version of the

Nesselrode and served it with rum-flavoured jam sauce. He also made a sundae, *coupe Yvette*, which was a bed of chopped *marrons glacés* and candied fruits, topped by a syrup-poached apricot surrounded by piped Chantilly cream, all kirsch-flavoured.

4–6 servings:

6 oz. (1 cup) marrons glacés
¼ pint (full ½ cup) double (heavy) cream
½ oz. (1 tablespoon) fine sugar
1 pint (2½ cups) vanilla ice cream

4 tablespoons (5) rum
4 oz. (1½ cups) crushed macaroons
for decoration:
Chantilly cream
marrons glacés

Sieve the chestnuts. Whip the cream and sugar stiffly. Combine the chestnuts and the cream with the ice cream. Sprinkle the rum on the macaroons. Fill a mould with alternate layers of the ice cream mixture and macaroons. Freeze until firm, about 5 hours. Turn out on to a chilled serving dish, pipe Chantilly cream on it and decorate with *marrons glacés*.

NESSELRODE PUDDING

This is one version of the famous pudding devised for a French count for whom it is named.

6–8 servings:

2 oz. (⅓ cup) currants
2 oz. (⅓ cup) sultanas
2 oz. (½ cup) candied orange peel
2 oz. (⅓ cup) glacé cherries
½ pint (1¼ cups) maraschino or rum or port
4 egg yolks
8 oz. (1 cup) fine sugar

1 pint (2½ cups) double (heavy) cream
4 oz. (⅔ cup) chestnut purée
for decoration:
¼ pint (full ½ cup) double (heavy) cream
½ oz. (1 tablespoon) fine sugar
1 tablespoon (1¼) maraschino
8 marrons glacés

Soak the currants and sultanas in warm water until they swell and chop the peel and cherries. Marinate all these fruits in the wine or spirit for at least an hour. Beat the egg yolks with 6 oz. (¾ cup) of the sugar until pale and fluffy. Heat three quarters of the cream but do not let it boil. Whisk it gradually into the egg and then stir the mixture continuously over gentlest heat – it must not boil – until it is thick enough to coat the back of the spoon. Remove from the heat and stir in the chestnut purée, the fruits and their marinade. Chill. Whip the rest of the cream with the rest of the sugar until stiff and

79

combine it thoroughly with the chilled mixture. Brush a mould lightly with sweet almond oil and pack in the pudding. Cover with foil and freeze until firm, 6 hours or more. Meantime, for the decoration, whip the cream, sugar and maraschino stiffly, pack into a piping bag and chill. When the mould is firm, dip its base momentarily in hot water. Remove the foil, cover the mould with a chilled serving dish and invert it. Pipe on the whipped cream and mount the *marrons glacés* in the piped cream.

BASIC BAVARIAN CREAM

Bavarian creams are also called *bavarois* (not to be confused with *bavaroise* which is a hot drink). Today these creams are normally bound with eggs but they can be made without them, using simply cream, gelatine and flavouring. Carême made them in the latter way including one flavoured by infusing the petals of 30 fresh-picked roses in 8 oz. (1 cup) sugar syrup.

Custard method
Make a basic custard (page 66) and stir in ½–¾ oz. (2–3 tablespoons) of dissolved gelatine, as it thickens. Cool it and when it begins to set, fold in ½ pint (1¼ cups) double (heavy) cream, lightly whipped, with flavouring and extra sugar to taste. Turn it into a mould rinsed in very cold water or brushed with sweet almond oil. Chill until set, turn out and serve.

Electric blender method
Blend ½ oz. (2 tablespoons) gelatine with ¼ pint (full ½ cup) hot liquid – fruit juice, strong coffee or flavoured milk, according to the type of cream wanted. Add 1 egg yolk, 1 oz. (2 tablespoons) sugar (or to taste) and ¼ pint (full ½ cup) fruit purée, strong coffee or milk and blend briefly. Add ¼ pint (full ½ cup) each of double (heavy) cream and crushed ice and blend until smooth. Pour the cream into a rinsed mould, chill it until set, turn it out gently and serve.

BAVARIAN CREAM VARIATIONS

Bavarian creams can take almost any flavour or colour. By dividing the custard in two before folding in the whipped cream you can build pink-and-white or chololate-and-white moulds. Set alternate layers of the plain half with layers of the other half incorporating 4 oz. (½ cup) raspberry or red-currant purée or 2 oz. (2 squares) chocolate melted and well stirred in – but let each layer set before adding another. Any of the moulds can be lined with caramelized sugar. They can also include 4 tablespoons (5) praline, 4 oz. ($\frac{2}{3}$ cup) *marrons glacés*, sieved and soaked in kirsch, or 2 oz. ($\frac{1}{3}$ cup) pounded nuts soaked in maraschino.

Shaped moulds can set off a dish when they are served surrounded by chopped jelly, poached fruits in syrup or fresh berry fruits set in Chantilly cream. My own preference with Bavarian creams however is not to unmould them but serve them in glass dishes. This method permits halving the amount of gelatine, which gives a more delicate texture. One may halve the gelatine too when these creams are used as fillings for flans or topping for other desserts, but not when they go into cold charlottes.

COLD CHARLOTTES

Cold charlottes are quite different from the hot fruit charlottes in chapter 3. Charlotte russe is traditionally made (Carême's way) with a Bavarian cream set in a straight-sided round mould which has been lined on base and sides with sponge fingers. The sponge fingers can be replaced by wafers or meringues, always with the flat side inward. The infinite variants in fillings can be almost any cream or custard thick enough to set firmly in these moulded sweets. Another variation, made with ice cream, is on page 93.

To prepare a charlotte mould, a round cake tin about 3 in. deep and of 2-pint (1$\frac{1}{2}$-quart) capacity is fine for 6–8 servings. Line the sides of the tin with sponge fingers trimmed so that they fit together closely all round. Sprinkle the base of the tin thickly with chopped nuts or, before lining the sides, line the base with sponge fingers cut to give a good cover in a pattern radiating from the centre of the base. Alternatively, one may put a little clear fruit jelly in the base, arrange a pattern of glacé cherries or other decoration in it and allow it to set. When the jelly has set line the sides with sponge fingers, fixing them to the base by dipping their ends in a little liquid jelly.

Whichever way you line the mould, fill it with Bavarian or other cream and chill it in the refrigerator. Unmould it when set and add further decorations, if you wish, of fruits (glacé or fresh), nuts, praline (page 76), marshmallows or piped cream.

LIQUEUR PECAN CHARLOTTE

Here is a cold charlotte made interesting with pecans or walnuts and enriched with liqueur. It will keep, covered, for several days in the refrigerator.

81

6 servings:

4 oz. (⅔ cup) pecans or walnuts	**¼ pint (full ½ cup) milk**
5½ oz. (⅔ cup) butter	**3 tablespoons (3¾) Grand**
5 oz. (full ½ cup) fine sugar	**Marnier**
1 egg yolk	**6 oz. boudoir biscuits**
½ teaspoon (⅔) instant coffee	**½ pint (1¼ cups) cream,**
powder	**whipped**
½ oz. (2 tablespoons) flour	**nuts to decorate**

Mince the nuts. Beat all but a tablespoon of the butter with the sugar until light and fluffy. Add the egg yolk, nuts and coffee powder. Melt the remaining butter in a small saucepan, blend in the flour, add half the milk gradually and stir well until the mixture is thick enough to leave the sides of the pan. Remove it from heat and leave to cool before beating it into the nut mixture with 2 tablespoons (2½) of the liqueur. Roll the biscuits quickly in the remaining milk and liqueur, mixed. Line the sides of a 6-in. Charlotte mould with biscuits and then line the bottom of the mould with the rest, cut to fit. Turn half the nut mixture into the mould, cover with a layer of biscuits and then add the rest of the nut mixture. Trim the ends of the biscuits level with the filling. Refrigerate for several hours before turning on to a chilled serving dish. Decorate the top with whirls of whipped cream, each topped with a blanched halved nut.

DIPLOMAT PUDDING, COLD

Much favoured in France for high days and holidays, cold *pouding diplomate* is, like the charlotte, made in a straight-sided mould. For this recipe a 2-pint (1½-quart) mould 3 in. deep is fine. Lightly brush the base and sides with sweet almond oil. As a variant, the hot diplomat pudding on page 66 can also be served cold.

6–8 servings:

18 sponge fingers (lady's	**1 Bavarian cream recipe**
fingers)	**(page 80)**
½ pint (1¼ cups) kirsch	**3 tablespoons (3¾) apricot jam**
2 oz. (½ cup) mixed candied	for the garnish:
fruits	**½ pint (1¼ cups) apricot glaze**
2 oz. (⅓ cup) sultanas	

Dip the sponge fingers in the kirsch. Chop the candied fruits and put them, with the sultanas, to soak in the kirsch. Trim 6 sponge fingers to points and arrange them with their curved sides down in radiating pattern on the base of the mould. Save the trimmings. Cover the base with a layer of partly set

Bavarian cream made by the custard method (page 80). Arrange more biscuits on the cream. Drain the fruits from the kirsch. Sprinkle some fruits on the biscuits and dot a teaspoon of jam here and there. Make layers in the order of cream, biscuits, fruit, using up the biscuit trimmings too. Refrigerate until set, about 5 hours. Strain the remaining kirsch and incorporate it with the glaze (page 123) ready for pouring over.

Turn the pudding out on to a chilled dish.

As an alternative to candied fruits and sultanas one may use berries or diced large fruits. Marinate them well in sugar and liqueur or spirit, draining them before setting them in the pudding.

DIPLOMAT PUDDING GARNISH

As a variant to a fruit glaze, try syrup-poached fruits (chapter 9). The poached peaches, pears, nectarines, apricots or cherries are set to cool while their syrup is thickened by further boiling. When cooled a little the syrup is enriched with kirsch, maraschino or other liqueur or spirit. Surround the pudding on its chilled serving dish with the fruit and pour the thick syrup over the fruit.

CREAM CHEESE DESSERTS

Unsalted cream cheese can be beaten with chopped candied fruits and the judicious addition of spices or other flavourings to make a quick dessert. It may also be beaten with a little fine sugar to serve with fruits instead of fresh cream.

The Italians use cream cheese (especially ricotta, traditionally made from ewe's milk) for many sweet as well as savoury dishes. I recommend particularly *ricotta al caffè* and the delicious summer cheese cake evolved by London's Good Housekeeping Institute.

COFFEE CREAM CHEESE

4 servings:

1 oz. ($\frac{1}{3}$ cup) freshly roasted coffee beans
10 oz. ($1\frac{1}{4}$ cups) cream cheese

6 oz. ($\frac{3}{4}$ cup) fine sugar
2 tablespoons ($2\frac{1}{2}$) rum

Grind the coffee beans to powder and sift it. Sieve the cream cheese and add the sugar, coffee and rum. Stir until it is smooth and thick and leave it for at least 2 hours in a cold place. Serve with fresh cream and wafer biscuits.

SUMMER CHEESE CAKE

10 servings:

¾ oz. (3 tablespoons) gelatine
6 oz. (¾ cup) fine sugar
pinch of salt
2 eggs, separated
½ pint (1¼ cups) milk
grated rind and juice ½ lemon
20 oz. (2½ cups) cottage cheese,
    sieved

¼ pint (full ½ cup) double
    (heavy) cream, whipped
8 oz. (1⅓ cups) strawberries
for crumb topping:
4 oz. (1 cup) digestive biscuits
½ oz. (1 tablespoon) fine sugar
1½ oz. (3 tablespoons) butter,
    melted

Blend together the gelatine, 5 oz. (full ½ cup) of the sugar and the salt. Beat the egg yolks and milk together and gradually stir them into the gelatine mixture. Stirring well, bring the mixture just to the boil and remove it from the heat. Add the grated lemon rind and strained juice and cool until it begins to set. Stir in the sieved cheese. Stiffly whisk the egg whites and fold them into the remaining sugar and the whipped cream. Put half the mixture in an 8-in.-base spring-release cake tin. Cover it with a layer of sliced strawberries and cover them with the rest of the cheese mixture. Crush the biscuits and blend them with the sugar and butter. Sprinkle the crumbs evenly over the cheese mixture and chill it until firm. Take the mould from the refrigerator a short time before turning it out carefully, crumb side down. Warm the mould's base slightly by putting a hot cloth on it to ensure it comes away easily. Serve the cake decorated with more strawberries.

CREAM CHEESE MOUSSE

6 servings:

4 eggs, separated
3 oz. (full ⅓ cup) fine sugar
6 oz. (¾ cup) cream cheese
¼ pint (full ½ cup) double
    (heavy) cream
3 tablespoons (3¾) Grand
    Marnier

for the sauce:
3 tablespoons (3¾) rum
4 tablespoons (5) water
3 oz. (½ cup) seedless raisins
1½ oz. (scant ⅓ cup) chopped
    mixed candied peel
1½ oz. (¼ cup) chopped glacé
    cherries

Beat the egg yolks with the sugar until creamy. Using a wire whisk, not a rotary one, gradually whisk in the cheese. Whip the cream and add it with the Grand Marnier or other orange-flavoured liqueur. Whisk the egg whites until stiff and fold them into the mixture. Turn the mixture into a large ice tray or two smaller ones and put it into the freezing compartment of the fridge but do *not* lower the temperature setting of the fridge as you would for ice cream. Leave it for several hours or overnight. To serve, spoon it into individual sundae glasses and add the sauce or hand it separately.

To make the sauce, bring the rum and water to the simmering point and then pour it over the raisins and mixed peel. Marinate for several hours. Stir in the chopped cherries just before serving. This dessert is particularly good made with *petit suisse* (using six individual ones) but any light cream cheese is suitable.

DESSERT JELLIES (SWEET GELATINES)

These are table jellies as distinct from jelly preserves which belong to jam-making. The gelatine used in these recipes is powdered gelatine which is dissolved in 2 or 3 (2½–3¾) tablespoons lukewarm water. Clear jellies should sparkle and to achieve maximum sparkle they are often clarified. Note that spirits or liqueurs are added to the jelly stock when it has cooled, just before it sets.

BASIC CLEAR JELLY

4 servings:

¾ oz. (3 tablespoons) gelatine, dissolved	2 cloves
1 pint (2½ cups) water	1 lemon
4 oz. (½ cup) sugar	1 orange
	white and shell of 1 egg

Put all the ingredients into a large saucepan. Whisking all the time, bring it slowly to the boil. Remove the whisk and let the jelly boil up with force. Remove it from the heat and let it settle for about 10 minutes. Strain it through a warm scalded cloth into a warmed basin if it is still not clear. When the jelly is nearly cold put it into a wet mould or moulds to set. Unmould it by loosening the edges with the finger tips, dipping the mould for a moment in hot water, then inverting the serving dish over the mould and turning the whole thing upside down.

CLARET JELLY

4 servings:

½ **pint (1¼ cups) water**	**1 bay leaf**
½ **pint (1¼ cups) claret**	**1 tablespoon (1¼) red currant**
rind of 1 lemon	**jelly (preserve)**
3 oz. (full ⅓ cup) sugar	**white and shell of 1 egg**
1 in. cinnamon stick	**¾ oz. (3 tablespoons) gelatine**

Make this jelly in the same way as the basic clear jelly (page 85) and add a little red colouring after straining it.

SHERRY JELLY

4 servings:

½ **pint (1¼ cups) water**	**1 in. cinnamon stick**
10 tablespoons (¾ cup) sherry	**2 cloves**
4 tablespoons (5) lemon juice	**white and shell of 1 egg**
rind of 1 lemon	**¾ oz. (3 tablespoons) gelatine**
3 oz. (full ⅓ cup) sugar	

Make this jelly in the same way as the basic clear jelly (page 85).

LIQUEUR JELLIES

For liqueur or spirit jelly, use the basic recipe (page 85) and when it is nearly cold stir in thoroughly 3 or 4 tablespoons (3¾–5) of curaçao, maraschino, Drambuie, Benedictine, rum or other spirit.

GINGER ALE JELLY

Make the basic clear jelly mixture (page 85) with 1 oz. (¼ cup) gelatine and ½ pint (1¼ cups) water, and when it is nearly cold add 1 pint (2½ cups) ginger ale or other clear soft drink.

CHOPPED JELLY

As a gay and tasty garnish for all sorts of cold sweets use a basic liqueur or wine clear jelly but increase the gelatine to 1 oz. (¼ cup). Turn it out on wet greaseproof or silicone paper and chop it coarsely with a wet knife. If you chop too finely it loses its clear sparkle.

FRUIT JELLIES (GELATINES)

With fruit juice
Substitute strained fruit juice (page 121) for the water in the basic clear jelly recipe (page 85). Note that fresh pineapple juice should be boiled for 5 minutes and cooled before being used with gelatine.

With fruit
Fresh fruit (of one kind or mixed) goes very well but cold poached or preserved fruit, well drained, can be good too. A wet mould embedded in crushed ice speeds the setting. Using the basic clear jelly recipe (page 85) or a wine or liqueur jelly recipe (page 86), cover the bottom of the mould with a little jelly liquid. When it is set dot it with the fruit or fruits and just cover them with more jelly liquid. When that is set add more fruit and more liquid – setting each layer before adding the next.

FRUIT CHARTREUSE

Line a straight-sided mould – first the base and then the sides – with clear jelly (page 85) and set in it whole berry fruits or other fruits sliced or diced. Set chopped pistachio nuts in between the fruit. Coat the inside with another thin layer of jelly and let it set. Fill the centre with a cream made by combining $\frac{1}{2}$ pint ($1\frac{1}{4}$ cups) double (heavy) cream, lightly whipped, with $\frac{1}{4}$ oz. (1 tablespoon) gelatine, dissolved, and $\frac{1}{4}$ pint (full $\frac{1}{2}$ cup) sweetened fruit purée. Chill to set and then unmould it.

JELLY WHIPS AND SNOWS

Since whipping destroys the sparkle, it is unnecessary to clarify jellies used in whips and snows. Omitting the clarifying process, all the jellies above are suitable for whips. The simplest whip is merely a jelly whisked to fluffiness when it is just beginning to set. It is then returned to a glass serving dish or individual glasses to be set and be served topped with fruit and/or cream or any suitable sauce. Also, one may incorporate $\frac{1}{4}$ pint (full $\frac{1}{2}$ cup) double (heavy) cream, whipped lightly, when whisking the jelly. For a jelly snow, fold in 2 stiffly whisked egg whites just before the jelly sets.

MARSHMALLOW

Marshmallows, either plain or toasted under the grill, can decorate almost any cold dessert or, cut up, they can be incorporated in creams or ice creams

87

to give texture contrast. They can be tinted with cochineal or other approved colourings. As variants in the recipe below, leave out the flower water and try a little oil of peppermint with green colouring, or 1½ tablespoons (2) grenadine (pomegranate) syrup with red or 1½ tablespoons (2) Cassis or other blackcurrant syrup.

10 oz. (1¼ cups) sugar	**1 egg white**
2 teaspoons (2½) glucose	**1½ tablespoons (2) orange-**
water	**flower or rose water**
¾ oz. (3 tablespoons) gelatine	

Dissolve the sugar and glucose in 4 tablespoons (5) water and boil to hard ball stage (260°F., 127°C.). Meantime warm ¼ pint (full ½ cup) water, dissolve the gelatine in it and keep it warm. Whisk the egg white stiffly. Whisking all the time, add the boiling syrup to the gelatine. Add the egg white and the flower water. Continue whisking until the mixture is thick and stiff. Pour it into a rectangular tin lined with greaseproof paper and dredged with icing sugar. When it is set cut it into 1-in. cubes with wet scissors. Roll the cubes in icing sugar and leave them to dry out overnight.

MARSHMALLOW SAUCE

8 oz. (1 cup) sugar	**pinch of salt**
3 tablespoons (4) water	**flavouring essence or syrup**
8 marshmallows (1-in. cubes)	**flavouring**
1 egg white	

Dissolve the sugar in the water and boil for 5 minutes. Cut up the marshmallows with wet scissors and stir them into the syrup with the salt, flavouring and, optionally, a colouring. Fold in the stiffly whisked egg white. Serve warm or cold.

This makes about ½ pint (1¼ cups) of sauce.

ice creams and iced puddings

Kings and emperors, princes and potentates were the Western world's pioneers of ice cream in the olden times before artificial refrigeration. It took a wealthy man to afford it. Even in the United States, apparently, a presidential dinner was needed to launch ice cream socially. It was a dinner given by President Madison in 1816 when custard pies, accidentally frozen in the ice box, nearly created a scandal but triumphed when the president's wife tried them and declared them delicious. Today the Americans are the world's champion ice-cream-eaters, and the ice cream, at its best, is highly nourishing and easily absorbed. The Americans eat more than three gallons each a year, three times the British average.

Making ice cream
Convenient though bought ice cream can be, it is easy to make at home and one can then have richer mixtures and one's own flavours and textures. The amount one can make in the ordinary refrigerator depends on the size of the ice-making compartment. Even a small compartment can take two $\frac{1}{2}$-pint ($1\frac{1}{4}$-cup) trays – with internal measurements of, say $6 \times 2\frac{1}{2} \times 1\frac{1}{2}$ in. One can measure tray capacity by filling the tray with water and pouring the water into a measuring jug. Rectangular plastic food containers, readily available in the shops, are useful for making ice cream or moulded iced sweets like Neapolitan ice gâteaux. Measure with a ruler the ice-making compartment and buy one that fits it.

Half an hour before making the ice cream, set the refrigerator to its coldest and put into it the whisking bowl needed for freezing the ice cream. The recipes below are for the ordinary refrigerator and since there are many variables, times given are approximate. A deep-freeze unit is obviously colder and freezing times will be reduced. As a rough guide, plan to re-whisk the ice cream 10 minutes after it goes into a deep-freeze unit and reckon that the ice cream will be ready to serve in about 30 minutes.

Flavours and colours for ice creams

The basic ice cream (or, indeed, water ices) can have any flavouring essence and, if wanted, colouring. Try oil of peppermint with green colour or raspberry essence with red, or use almond essence with 2 tablespoons (2½) chopped almonds or praline. Pistachio ice cream often has vanilla essence, 2–3 tablespoons (2½–3¾) chopped pistachios and green colouring. Chocolate ice cream is the basic recipe with 2 oz. (2 squares) melted chocolate stirred in while the custard is cooking. For coffee ice cream use coffee essence or 2 tablespoons (2½) treble-strength black coffee or cook 4 oz. (1⅓ cups) crushed freshly roasted coffee beans with the custard and leave them in it, stirring frequently, for 1 hour before straining it into the ice tray.

Liqueur ice creams. In the basic ice cream recipe (page 91) omit the flavouring essence and add 1 tablespoon (1¼) liqueur with, optionally, colouring to match (green with crème de menthe or green chartreuse, red with cherry brandy etc.).

Sauces for ices and ice creams

Straight syrups of fruits or ginger make excellent sauces, simply poured on to the ice cream or water ice. The strongly-coloured ones, such as pomegranate, blackcurrant, redcurrant and mulberry can add eye appeal as well as flavour. Straight liqueurs can be used in the same way.

Almost any dessert sauce goes well with water ices. Ice creams are often best accompanied by the less creamy sauces or simply by sweetened fruit purées. Pleasing contrast can be achieved with a hot sauce – say, the chocolate cream sauce (page 136) or zabaglione (page 74).

A simple chocolate sauce for ice creams is made this way. Melt 4 oz. (4 squares) dark chocolate and 1 oz. (2 tablespoons) butter in a basin over a pan of hot water. Stir in 2 tablespoons (2½) of vanilla-flavoured milk and serve straight away over the ice cream.

Equally easy is a coffee-caramel sauce. To make it, dissolve 8 oz. (1 cup) fine sugar in a pan over moderate heat and then increase the heat to brown it a little. Slowly add ½ pint (1¼ cups) of freshly-made strong black coffee; stir and boil for about 5 minutes. Cool it slightly but serve it still warm. This is very good with a lemon-flavoured ice.

At one of my favourite little Swiss restaurants they serve strong unsweetened black coffee hot as a sauce. Although they call it *café glacé Edelweiss*, it is a dessert eaten with a long spoon. Into a tall chilled glass they put a good scoopful of firm coffee ice cream and top it with a piped swirl of whipped cream before adding a demi-tasse of hot coffee. You can paint the lily, if you like, by putting rum in the coffee or Tia Maria in the cream.

BASIC ICE CREAM

The recipe here is described as for 4 servings on the assumption that there will be generous accompaniments of sauce, fruit or such. Obviously the ingredients should be doubled up without them or if one is serving it to ice-cream enthusiasts. An economical version of basic ice cream for 4 servings uses ¼ pint (full ½ cup) double (heavy) cream, ¼ pint (full ½ cup) milk, 1½ oz. (3 tablespoons) sugar and 1 beaten egg, prepared as in the recipe below. Similarly one can substitute single cream for double cream in the recipe below.

4 servings:

4 egg yolks
3 oz. (full ⅓ cup) sugar

½ pint (1¼ cup) double (heavy) cream
flavouring essence

Set the refrigerator to its coldest point and put in it a bowl to chill. Beat the egg yolks with the sugar and then the cream. Add the flavouring essence. Stir the mixture over very gentle heat until it thickens, making certain that it does not boil. Strain it into a bowl and stir it frequently as it cools. When cool, pour it into the ice tray or trays and put it into the ice-making compartment of the refrigerator. When it is half-frozen (in 30–40 minutes) turn it into the chilled bowl, whisk it quickly and thoroughly and return it to the tray in the ice compartment. It should be firm and ready in about 2 hours.

AVOCADO ICE CREAM

6–8 servings:

2 eggs
8 oz. (1 cup) fine sugar
1 pint (2½ cups) vanilla-flavoured milk

2 medium-size avocado pears
lime or lemon peel

Set the refrigerator to its lowest temperature and put in a bowl to chill. Whisk the eggs, half the sugar and all the milk in a bowl over hot water until the custard thickens. Leave it to cool. Mix the remaining sugar with the flesh of the avocado pears and beat well. Blend the beaten pear flesh into the custard. Put the mixture into a freezing tray and freeze it until mushy. Remove it from the refrigerator, beat it in the chilled bowl and return it to the freezing compartment. When it is really firm serve it in individual glass dishes garnished with a grating of lime or lemon peel.

FRUIT ICE CREAMS

For 6 servings, sieve 1 lb. strawberries, apricots or other fruit and combine with the cooled custard in the basic ice cream recipe (page 91).

Also, one may simply combine $\frac{1}{2}$ pint ($1\frac{1}{4}$ cups) fruit juice or purée with $\frac{1}{2}$ pint ($1\frac{1}{4}$ cups) double (heavy) cream whipped with 3 oz. (full $\frac{1}{3}$ cup) sugar. Freeze the mixture in ice trays for 2–3 hours, stirring it every half-hour or so. For the melon ice cream below I prefer the sweet little round Charentais melons but alternatives are two Ogen melons or one honeydew.

For *tutti frutti* ice cream use the basic recipe (page 91) and add to the cooled custard 2 tablespoons ($2\frac{1}{2}$) each of chopped nuts, glacé cherries and angelica.

CHARENTAIS ICE CREAM

2 ripe Charentais melons
4 oz. ($\frac{1}{2}$ cup) sugar
juice of 1 lemon
$\frac{1}{2}$ pint ($1\frac{1}{4}$ cups) double (heavy) cream

1 tablespoon ($1\frac{1}{4}$) Drambuie
8 amaretti (page 130)

Halve the melons by cutting through the girth line. Remove the seeds and scoop out the flesh, carefully preserving the melon shell intact. Put the shells in the refrigerator. Put the flesh in a pan with 3 oz. (full $\frac{1}{3}$ cup) sugar (or to taste) and warm it over a low heat until the sugar is dissolved and the melon soft enough to go through a sieve. Add the lemon juice and let the fruit cool. Sieve it. Whip the cream with 1 oz. (2 tablespoons) sugar and the Drambuie (or Benedictine or other liqueur). Fold the cream into the fruit and freeze the mixture, stirring it up after 30 minutes and again after 90 minutes. Stick two amaretti like butterfly wings in the top of each melon half just before serving.

SNOWY ICE CREAM

For flavouring in this lighter ice cream use a little essence or 1 tablespoon fortified wine or spirit. It goes well served on top of pineapple or other fruit. Or you can serve it in glasses topped with kirsch-soaked chopped fruit or nuts.

4 servings:
2 egg whites
$1\frac{1}{2}$ oz. (full $\frac{1}{3}$ cup) icing (confectioners') sugar

$\frac{1}{4}$ pint (full $\frac{1}{2}$ cup) double (heavy) cream
flavouring

Whip the egg whites stiffly and sieve the sugar. Whip the cream until it is thick but not stiff adding the sugar, flavouring and then the egg whites. Pour it into the ice tray and freeze for 2–3 hours re-whisking it in a chilled bowl after half an hour.

MALLOW CREAMS

For variations in the following recipe leave out the strawberries and orange juice and substitute ¼ pint (full ½ cup) of fruit juice or purée, or of treble-strength black coffee, or of milk with 2 oz. (2 squares) chocolate dissolved in it.

6 servings:

½ **lb. strawberries**	**20 marshmallows, 1-in. cubes**
1 tablespoon (1¼) orange juice	**4 tablespoons (5) water**
2 oz. (½ cup) icing	**½ pint (1¼ cups) double**
(confectioners') sugar	**(heavy) cream**

Set the refrigerator to coldest. Crush the strawberries with a fork, mix them with the orange juice and sugar and leave them for 30 minutes. Stir the marshmallows in the water over a pan of hot water until dissolved. Remove them from the heat and add the strawberries. When the mixture is cold and slightly stiff, lightly whip the cream and fold it into the strawberry mixture. Pour the mixture into an ice tray or trays and freeze it, without stirring, until it is firm, 2–3 hours.

EDWARDIAN ICE CREAM

I am indebted to Sheila Hutchins for this ice cream which, as she points out, 'is made of all things from brown breadcrumbs and dead simple to make in the domestic refrigerator'. It is best made in the morning to be sure it is set for dinner. Stale crumbs from a rough wholewheat loaf give it a good nutty flavour. Turn the refrigerator to maximum cold in advance. Mix 4 oz. (2⅔) cups breadcrumbs with ½ pint (1¼ cups) double cream, stiffly whipped, and 3 oz. (full ⅓ cup) vanilla-flavoured fine sugar. Put it in the ice-making compartment of the refrigerator. When it is half frozen whip it up in a chilled bowl and add 1 tablespoon (1¼) rum or brandy. Return it to the freezing compartment for at least 3 hours.

ICED CHARLOTTE RUSSE

There are hot charlottes in chapter 3 and cold in chapter 6. Here is yet another, made with ice cream. A home-freezer is needed to make the charlotte but the recipe is good too for a sundae made by serving the ice creams in individual glasses with sherry syrup spooned over and the sponge fingers (lady's fingers) served separately.

12 servings:

vanilla ice cream:
½ pint (1¼ cups) milk
3 oz. (full ⅓ cup) sugar
1 vanilla pod
2 eggs, beaten
½ pint (1¼ cups) double
   (heavy) cream
raspberry ice cream:
1 pint (2½ cups) water
12 oz. (1½ cups) sugar

1 lb. raspberries
8 tablespoons (10) lemon juice
12 oz. (full 1¼ cups) hazelnut
   yoghurt
sponge case:
3 tablespoons (3¾) sugar
4 tablespoons (5) water
4 tablespoons (5) sherry
28 sponge fingers (lady's
   fingers) or boudoir biscuits

To prepare the vanilla ice cream put a bowl in the refrigerator to chill and heat the milk with the sugar and the vanilla pod. Stirring well, pour the milk on to the eggs. Return the mixture to the saucepan and cook over low heat, stirring, until the custard thickens. Strain the custard, removing the vanilla pod. Allow the custard to cool. Half whip the cream and fold it into the cold custard. Freeze the mixture in an ice tray until mushy. Turn it into the chilled bowl, whisk it thoroughly and return it to freeze again until mushy.

To prepare the raspberry ice cream, dissolve the sugar in the water, bring it to the boil and reduce it to 1 pint (2½ cups). Cool it. Sieve the berries and add the lemon juice, yoghurt and sugar syrup. Turn it into an ice tray and freeze it to a mush.

For the sponge case, crumple up aluminium foil and form it into a collar to fit around the inside of an 8½-in. round cake tin, leaving a slight space to take the sponge fingers. Dissolve the sugar in the water in a small pan and simmer for 5 minutes. Cool it and blend it with the sherry in a flat dish. Soak the sponge fingers briefly in the sherry syrup, removing them before they soften. Stand them in the gap between the tin's side and the foil. Layer the vanilla and raspberry ice creams, starting with half the vanilla. Lift the foil ring as the vanilla layer is spooned in but leave the foil in position above the vanilla layer to support the sponge fingers. Freeze this vanilla layer. Remove the foil. Make another layer with half of the raspberry ice cream, freeze and add another vanilla layer. Freeze, add the final raspberry layer and freeze again. Turn the charlotte out and serve it in wedges, cutting it with a knife dipped in warm water.

WATER ICES, SHERBETS AND SPOOMS

Ices without egg yolks and cream are as varied in definition as in their recipes. For straight water ices the refrigerator is best set in advance to its coldest temperature. The granulated water ice the Italians call *granita*, the sherbet and the spoom (from the Italian *spuma*, froth or spray) are not frozen solid and can be set at the refrigerator's normal ice-making temperature. Most of these desserts use sugar syrup.

SUGAR SYRUP FOR ICES

Dissolve 8 oz. (1 cup) sugar in 1 pint (2½ cups) water and bring it to the boil. Boil it gently for 10 minutes (to 220°F., 104°C.) and remove it from the heat. Add the juice of ½ lemon and let it cool.

COFFEE ICE

4 servings:

1 pint (2½ cups) water　　　　**2 oz. (¼ cup) sugar**
4 oz. (1⅓ cups) finely ground　　**1 egg white**
**　coffee**

Set the refrigerator to the coldest point. Boil the water and pour it over the coffee and sugar in a jug. Leave the jug for 30 minutes in a pan of hot (not boiling) water over the gentlest heat. Let it cool and strain the coffee through a cloth. Pour it into ice tray or trays and put it into the freezer. When the coffee is half-frozen (about 30 minutes) put it into a well-chilled bowl, beat in the stiffly-whisked egg white and return it to the ice tray. Freeze it until firm but not too hard (about 2½ hours), stirring it from time to time. Serve it in glasses topped with lightly whipped cream sweetened to taste.

FRUIT ICES

For 4 servings mix ½ pint (1¼ cups) cold sugar syrup with ½ pint (1¼ cups) fruit juice or purée. Proceed as for coffee ice (above), adding the whisked egg white when the mixture is half-frozen. For banana and strawberry ices, add the juice of 1 orange to the purée.

For lemon, orange, tangerine or grapefruit ices, stir into the mixed fruit flesh, juice and syrup the grated rind of 3 lemons (or equivalent of other rind) and leave the mixture for 3 hours before straining it through cloth.

95

These mixtures are often served in the emptied fruit skin. Cut the top third off the fruit, scoop out the inside completely and chill the empty skins – ideally in a deep-freeze unit to give them a real frost coating. Spoon in the ice when it is ready.

For cherry or apricot ice, crush 1 lb. stoned cherries (or apricots) or put them briefly through the electric blender. Crush the kernels, add them to the syrup and leave them for an hour or two before sieving them.

GRANITA

The *granita* (in France, *granité*) is made with any water ice recipe minus the egg white. Stirring it from time to time in the ice tray speeds the freezing but it does not need to be re-whisked since the little ice crystals are its character. Serve it plain in glasses. If you put a lemon *granité* in old wood-matured Calvados you have a *trou normand*, a draught to be taken between the richer savoury courses of a banquet or a big family dinner party. The *trou* is more usually nowadays replaced by a *sorbet* or sherbet.

SHERBETS

Sherbets (in France, *sorbets*) can be served as palate-refreshers in the middle of a meal but more often they make excellent light desserts, with or without other cold sweets. They can be simply soft water ices, the softness being achieved by adding 1 extra stiffly-whisked egg white to the fruit ice recipes above. A sophisticated sherbet is made with wine or laced with liqueur or spirit. Port, sweet sherry or Frontignan are good.

Wine-based sherbet. For 4 servings, mix $\frac{1}{2}$ pint ($1\frac{1}{4}$ cups) wine with the juice of 1 lemon and 1 orange and $\frac{3}{4}$ pint (scant 2 cups) cold sugar syrup. Put the mixture to freeze for about 1 hour. In a well-chilled bowl fold into it 2 stiffly-whisked egg whites and quickly return the mixture to freeze until firm but not hard. Spoon it into goblets and sprinkle it with wine or liqueur.

Sherbet with liqueur. Make the wine-based sherbet with only $\frac{1}{4}$ pint (full $\frac{1}{2}$ cup) wine and when it is frozen beat into it 3 tablespoons ($3\frac{3}{4}$) liqueur.

SPOOMS AND SPUMONI

Spooms are sherbets, usually wine-based, with 4 stiffly-whisked egg whites instead of 2, and $\frac{1}{2}$ pint ($1\frac{1}{4}$ cups) sugar syrup instead of $\frac{3}{4}$ pint (scant 2 cups). Try champagne or a sweet bordeaux as the wine.

Spumoni are richer, being made with cream. They can incorporate chopped fruit (strawberries go well) or purées, chopped nuts or candied fruits.

RASPBERRY SPUMONI (*Illustrated*)

4 servings:

1 lb. raspberries	**½ pint (1¼ cups) double**
1 oz. (2 tablespoons) fine sugar	**(heavy) cream**
juice of ½ lemon	**1 oz. (¼ cup) icing**
	(confectioners') sugar

Sieve the raspberries and mix them well with the sugar and lemon juice. Whip the cream stiffly, fold in the icing sugar and fold the cream into the raspberry purée. Pack the mixture into a mould and chill in the freezer until it is firmly set.

NEAPOLITAN ICE GÂTEAUX

Not Naples, but a French chef of England's King Charles I is credited with the invention of Neapolitan ices. The chef returned to Paris after the luckless king's execution and sold his rainbow mixture to the Café Napolitain – whence the name. Commercially the *cassata* is sometimes confused with the Neapolitan but its most authentic version is a form of *bombe* (page 99).

Into a well-chilled rectangular mould pack layers of half-frozen ices or ice creams. Use different ice creams or ices for adjoining layers – say white praline, pink raspberry, brown chocolate, green mint or pistachio. Freeze the block for 2–3 hours, turn it out and cut it in slices to serve unadorned or decorated, with or without a sauce. Layers of vanilla and coffee ice cream alternating with orange sherbet make a delightful combination.

COMTESSE MARIE ICE CREAM

Line a square mould with half-frozen strawberry ice cream, fill it with half-frozen vanilla ice cream and freeze it for 2–3 hours. Unmould and decorate it with whole strawberries marinaded in kirsch. Alternatively, line the mould with strawberry ice, sherbet or *granité*, fill it with chilled vanilla-flavoured whipped cream and freeze it for 2–2½ hours.

SUNDAES AND COUPES

The French call sundaes *coupes* for the logical reason that they are served in cups, of silver or glass. Dictionaries disagree on the origin of the word sundae.

The version I like is that Illinois banned ice cream on Sundays but finally agreed that an ice cream wasn't an ice cream if it was topped with nuts and fruit – hence the Sundae Ice. Sundaes and *coupes* can be based on ices or ice creams.

COUPE JACQUES (*Illustrated*)

This is the classic French *coupe glacée* – spoon alternate spoonfuls of lemon and raspberry ices into glasses with a couple of tablespoonsfuls of diced kirsch-soaked fruit, fresh or crystallized, between. It can be decorated with glacé cherries and blanched green almonds and sprinkled with kirsch.

ICED MOUSSES, PARFAITS AND BOMBES

Almost any mousse mixture which does not contain gelatine can be frozen rather than merely chilled. Fruit and other flavoured mousses are often used as a filling for *bombes* (page 99).

FROZEN COFFEE MOUSSE

4 servings:

6 tablespoons (7½) treble-strength black coffee	3 oz. (full ⅓ cup) fine sugar
4 eggs, separated	½ pint (1¼ cups) double (heavy) cream

Put the coffee, egg yolks and sugar into a large bowl over a pan of hot water and whisk them until thick and creamy. Remove the mixture from the heat and continue whisking until cold. Fold in the cream, whipped, and the stiffly-whisked egg whites. Pour the mixture into a mould or individual dishes and freeze as for ice cream (pages 89, 91).

ICED FRUIT MOUSSES

Combine ¼ pint (full ½ cup) sugar syrup (as for ices on page 95), with an equal quantity of fruit juice or purée and ½ pint (1¼ cups) double (heavy) cream, whipped. Put the mixture into ice tray or trays and freeze as for ice cream. Like fruit ices, these mousses can go to table in the shells, carefully scooped out, of their 'mother' fruits. Try iced pineapple mousse spooned into its well-chilled shell with the spiky green top as a lid. Now that one can buy quite tiny pineapples, one may even serve a whole one per person.

BUTTERSCOTCH PARFAIT

Rich and mousse-like in texture, parfaits were originally made only as iced coffee-flavoured desserts. Nowadays they are of rum, brandy, chocolate, ginger, praline and many other flavours.

4 servings:

4 egg yolks
1 oz. (2 tablespoons) butter
3 oz. (full ⅓ cup) brown sugar
¼ pint (full ½ cup) hot water

½ pint (1¼ cups) double (heavy) cream
flavouring essence

Beat the egg yolks until pale and frothy. Melt the butter and sugar and boil them for 1 minute. Add the water and stir until the butterscotch is dissolved. Reduce the heat to minimum and gradually add the egg yolks, stirring for 5 minutes but making sure the mixture does not boil. Remove it from the heat and let it cool. Fold in the whipped cream and essence and freeze as for ice cream.

BOMBES

Bombes were named for the spherical moulds in which they were first shaped. Today a pudding basin is more common or for want of something better any shape of mould will do. Basically a *bombe* is a shell of an ice or ice cream filled, usually, with a mousse or parfait mixture of complementary or contrasting flavour. But the centre can just as well be of another ice or ice cream or of Chantilly cream or layers of different fillings. Both shell and filling can incorporate diced fruit, fresh or crystallized, crushed macaroons, flaked chocolate, chopped angelica, ginger, *marrons glacés* or blanched green nuts. Optionally, serve a *bombe* with a liqueur-flavoured or syrup-flavoured pouring cream or a sauce on the side. As an example, for 8–10 servings, incorporate 2 oz. (2 squares) flaked or chopped chocolate or chocolate vermicelli in the basic ice cream (page 91) flavoured with vanilla. When it is half-frozen line a well-chilled mould (ideally, a mould set in crushed ice) with it, pressing it firmly against the mould. Pack in firmly a well-chilled apricot mousse mixture flavoured with rum or maraschino. Slightly over-fill the mould and press the top down flat. Cover it with waxed paper and then with foil. Freeze it for 2–3 hours. Dip the mould in tepid water for a few seconds, remove the foil and paper and turn out the *bombe* on to a cold serving dish.

The serving dish should be thoroughly chilled and the *bombe* will have better insulation if it is turned out on to a bed of chopped jelly (page 86) or a sponge. Using the basic true sponge recipe (page 143) make a sponge about

1 in. bigger all round than the *bombe*. Brush the sponge with sieved apricot jam and roll the sides in chopped nuts. Decorate the top edge of the sponge with piped whipped cream or rum-flavoured Chantilly cream.

SICILIAN CASSATA

There is some confusion between the traditional refrigerated cheese cake called *cassata alla Siciliana* and the *bombe* type ice-cream dish rightly called *cassata gelata*, so I have included both recipes.

6 servings:

12 oz. (1½ cups) ricotta or fresh cream cheese

6 oz. (¾ cup) vanilla-flavoured sugar

4 oz. (4 squares) bitter chocolate

4 oz. (1 cup) candied fruit

2 oz. (⅓ cup) pistachio nuts

4 oz. sponge fingers (lady's fingers)

2 tablespoons (2½) maraschino

Sieve the cheese. Beat in the sugar until the mixture is smooth and fluffy. Chop up the chocolate with half the candied fruit and the nuts and mix them well with the cheese. Line a bowl with the sponge fingers, trimming where needed to get a good cover, and sprinkle on the maraschino. Pack in the ricotta mixture and refrigerate, covered, for 3 hours or more. Invert a chilled plate over the bowl and turn bowl and plate upside down. Remove the bowl and decorate the cake with slices of the rest of the candied fruit.

CASSATA GELATA

6 servings:

2 basic ice cream recipes (page 91)

2 tablespoons (2½) marsala

1 oz. toasted hazel nuts (scant ¼ cup) or almonds

2 oz. (½ cup) candied fruit

Prepare the basic ice cream using twice the quantities of each ingredient and blending in the marsala. Chop finely the nuts and candied fruits (say, cherries, lemon or orange peel and angelica) and mix them into the ice cream before freezing. Freeze for at least 2 hours, stirring after the first 30 minutes.

ICE CREAM-MERINGUE DESSERTS

Meringues glacées, meringue shells sandwiched with ice cream and topped with whipped cream, are always an enticing dessert. Decorate them, optionally, with sugar-frosted violets (page 152). You can also scoop out the shells on the flat side and put in a spoonful of blackberry or redcurrant jam before sandwiching them with the ice cream.

BAKED ALASKA

Among the popular desserts to which ice cream is essential is the baked Alaska. The name is often appropriated for other meringue surprise dishes (like the melon Alaska on page 127). Here is what we may call the authorized version. It is also called Norwegian omelette. Using the basic ice cream recipe (page 91) or any of the flavoured variations, freeze it until it has set very hard. For 4–6 servings, put a sponge flan case (about 7 in. in diameter) on a larger flat oven-proof dish. Sprinkle the sponge with 2–3 tablespoons ($2\frac{1}{2}$–$3\frac{3}{4}$) sherry, madeira or other fortified wine or spirit. Pre-heat the oven to very hot (475°F., mark 9). Make a meringue with 4 egg whites and 8 oz. (1 cup) vanilla-flavoured fine sugar. Put the ice cream on the sponge base and cover it and the sponge down to the edge of the plate with meringue, swirling it into peaks. Sprinkle it with a little fine sugar and, if you like, a dusting of cinnamon. Put it into a hot oven for about 5 minutes, until it colours slightly, and serve it forthwith.

MERINGUE SURPRISE

Make a biscuit-crumb flan case (page 56) and chill it well. Fill it with firm-frozen ice cream and add a layer of chilled sliced poached peaches, apricots or nectarines. Completely cover the top with meringue and colour it under a very hot grill. Banana frost-and-fire (page 127) is another form of meringue surprise.

batter sweets and omelettes

Fried desserts like pancakes and sweet omelettes include such gastronomic delights that they cannot be denied. Admittedly, however, they are more suitable for meals with the family and close friends unless you have staff to prepare them and a kitchen you can efficiently shut off, since not everyone appreciates the smell of frying. I, on the other hand, have never found this a problem in those wonderful little pancake shops of Normandy, the *crêperies*, where they prepare their wafer-thin *crêpes* right there beside you. The combination of spotlessly clean equipment and fresh olive oil (and the thinnest possible brushing of it, at that) makes a fragrance that whets the appetite to impatience. Pancakes which are going to be heated in a sauce – *crêpes Suzette*, for instance – can, anyhow, be made hours or days in advance, stacked flat between sheets of waxed paper and stored in a cool larder or the refrigerator.

Pancakes, fritters, blinis, blintzes, waffles, clafoutis, the Scots' sooty bannocks and drop scones – a host of golden offerings are made with batter. Batter mixtures should always be beaten well and the cooking should be swift. With exceptions noted in individual recipes, it is not necessary to mix batters hours in advance but when that is more convenient cover the batter and leave it in a cold place. Give it a last beating immediately before cooking.

There are two main types of batter. One, as thin as single cream, is for all kinds of pancakes and for most batter puddings. The other is thicker, of a coating consistency, for fritters and waffles.

PANCAKES

Pancakes, which the French call *crêpes*, should be cooked in a really heavy-based shallow frying pan with sloping sides. A pan with a base diameter of about 6 in. is good for most pancakes. It should be thoroughly hot and only lightly greased. I simply brush the hot pan with olive oil. To keep pancakes warm as they are made, pile them on a plate over a pan of hot water if you like them soft. If you want them crisper, put them in the oven to keep warm. Quantities in the basic recipe (below) make about ten thin pancakes in a 6-in. pan. The simplest of English pancake batters is: 4 oz. (1 cup) plain flour, a pinch of salt, 1 egg, $\frac{1}{2}$ pint (1$\frac{1}{4}$ cups) milk or milk and water. I prefer the following slightly richer French batter.

BASIC PANCAKES

4 servings:

4 oz. (1 cup) plain flour　　　　　$\frac{1}{2}$ **pint (1$\frac{1}{4}$ cups) milk**
pinch of salt　　　　　　　　　　　$\frac{1}{2}$ **oz. (1 tablespoon) butter,**
2 eggs　　　　　　　　　　　　　　　**melted**

Sieve the flour and salt into a mixing bowl. Make a well in the centre and break in the eggs. Work them until the mixture is thoroughly amalgamated.

Gradually add the milk and melted butter, stirring with a wooden spoon, and continue beating well until air bubbles have formed on top and all is smooth and of the consistency of thin cream. Brush the base and sides of a hot pan with oil simply to give it a gloss. Pour 2 tablespoons (2$\frac{1}{2}$) of the batter into the centre of the pan, tilting so that it evenly covers the base. Cook quickly until it is golden on one side (about 1 minute). Turn it with a spatula or palette knife – or deftly toss it – and cook the second side for another minute. Turn out flat on a warm plate. Brush the pan with oil again before making each pancake.

PANCAKE FINISHES

For Shrove Tuesday pancakes, sprinkle each with fine sugar and lemon juice, roll it up and serve it with a lemon wedge and more caster sugar – ideally, as soon as each is made. Try cinnamon sugar as a variant. Stuffed pancakes (called *pannequets* in France) have highly variable fillings from warmed jam to fruit or chestnut purée, spread before the pancakes are rolled up. The rolled or folded pancakes can be put on a hot ovenproof dish or baking sheet, topped with sugar and finely-chopped almonds or pistachio nuts and quickly glazed under the grill or in a fierce oven.

ENRICHED PANCAKE BATTERS

For a richer batter add 2 egg yolks, an extra whole egg, or 2 tablespoons ($2\frac{1}{2}$) double (heavy) cream to either of the basic pancake recipes. The contrast of an unsweetened pancake with a sweet filling is, for me, one of the charms of dessert pancakes but, for those who like them sweeter, add 1 oz. (2 tablespoons) fine sugar with the flour and salt, and a tablespoon of brandy, rum or a liqueur or syrup. For variation of texture, separate the eggs, beating the yolks into the batter and then folding in the stiffly whisked whites when the batter is smooth and creamy or add a tablespoon of crushed macaroons.

NORMANDY PANCAKES

4 servings:

basic pancake batter | **3 tablespoons ($3\frac{3}{4}$) blanched**
(page 103) | **and chopped almonds**
3 eating apples | **4–6 tablespoons (5–$7\frac{1}{2}$) double**
1 oz. (2 tablespoons) butter | **(heavy) cream, whipped**
juice of $\frac{1}{2}$ lemon | **3 tablespoons ($3\frac{3}{4}$) Calvados**
3 tablespoons ($3\frac{3}{4}$) apricot jam | **fine sugar**

Make the batter. Peel, core and dice the apples and cook them with the butter and lemon juice until tender. While they are cooking make 10 thin pancakes, stack them flat and keep warm. Stir the jam and almonds into the apples and then fold in the cream blended with the Calvados. Spread this mixture on each pancake and roll it up or fold it in four. Put them in a shallow buttered ovenproof dish, sprinkle with fine sugar and glaze under the grill for a minute or so. Serve immediately.

CRÊPES SUZETTE

As André Simon pointed out, 'there are practically as many different types of pancakes bearing the name of *crêpes Suzette* as there are *maîtres d'hôtel* to make them'. There are also as many legends as to their origin. One says they were christened by England's King Edward VII, another that they were first created for King Louis XV of France. With M. Simon I accept that they were introduced in an 1897 Paris play, served by a maid called Suzette, and were flavoured 'with orange juice and naught else'. However, most people nowadays would feel deprived if their *crêpes Suzette* did not contain orange-flavoured liqueur and were not flamed with brandy, so this is the version I give. The liqueur is usually one of the curaçaos like Cointreau, Triple Sec, Van der Hum or Grand Marnier.

4 servings:

basic pancake batter (page 103)	**juice of 2 oranges**
2 oz. ($\frac{1}{4}$ cup) butter	**grated rind of 1 lemon**
2 oz. (scant $\frac{1}{2}$ cup) icing	**4 tablespoons (5) curaçao**
(confectioners') sugar	**2 tablespoons ($2\frac{1}{2}$) brandy**

Grease the frying pan – this time with butter. Make the pancakes and stack them flat. Cream the butter and icing sugar together and add the orange juice, lemon rind and half of the curaçao. Gently heat this butter in the frying pan (or chafing dish at table) until it bubbles, about 5 minutes. Dip each cooked pancake into the butter, fold it into quarters and push it to one side of the pan. Finally, add the remaining curaçao and the brandy to the pan, stand back and ignite the liquid with a match or, better, a taper. Spoon the flaming pan sauce over the pancakes and serve them with the sauce as soon as the flames subside.

LEMON CREAM PANCAKES

4 servings:

basic pancake batter (page 103)	**grated rind of 1 lemon**
filling:	**3 level tablespoons ($3\frac{3}{4}$) fine**
$\frac{1}{4}$ pint (full $\frac{1}{2}$ cup) double	**sugar**
(heavy) cream, whipped	**1 tablespoon ($1\frac{1}{4}$) curaçao**
2 tablespoons ($2\frac{1}{2}$) lemon juice	

Make and stack the pancakes. Blend well together the ingredients for the filling. Put a good spoonful on each pancake – it spreads itself – and roll each up to serve immediately.

BLINTZES

Blini and blintzes have much in common. Blini is the plural of *blin*, Russian for pancake, and blintz or blintze comes from *blintse*, the Yiddish form of the Russian diminutive of *blin*. Often made with a buckwheat batter these small pancakes can come in savoury form with fillings ranging from caviar to well-seasoned mashed potatoes. For the dessert versions, alternative fillings include jam or fruit purée combined with cream cheese or cottage cheese.

4 servings:
basic pancake batter (page 103)
for the filling:
4 oz. (½ cup) cottage cheese
2 tablespoons (2½) sour cream
1 egg, beaten
grated rind of 1 lemon

1 tablespoon (1¼) icing
(confectioners') sugar
for the garnish:
cinnamon sugar
sour cream, chilled

Combine the ingredients for the filling. Cook the pancakes rather lightly in butter. Spread the filling on them and fold over the two sides to enclose it. Grease the pan again and return the blintzes to it and cook until crisp and golden. Dust with cinnamon sugar and serve very hot with sour cream.

FRITTERS

The French come persistently into the fritter story because over the centuries they have developed fritters in almost infinite variety and many of their recipes have been handed down for generations by word of mouth. The French word for fritter, *beignet*, is said to derive from an old word meaning to swell. And this is indeed what fritter batter should do in the cooking – puff up so that it is light, golden and crisp while the food it encloses is succulent and soft. Some say though that *beignet* comes from *baigner*—a reasonable argument as we do make fritters by dipping or bathing them in the transforming hot oil.

A fritter is any food coated with batter (or sometimes paste or dough) and quickly deep-fried in very hot oil or cooking fat (not butter). The cooking of the food and the puffing of the batter coating is effected by the boiling of the moisture in the food. The temperature of the oil is important. For most fritters it is between 370°F. and 380°F. (188°C. and 195°C.) for which a simple test is that it will brown a 1-in. cube of bread in 40 seconds. Occasionally moderately hot oil is used – say, around 350°F. (177°C.) – which takes 60 seconds or just over to brown the bread cube.

FRITTER BATTER—1

4 servings:
4 oz. (1 cup) plain flour
pinch of salt
¼ pint (full ½ cup) warm water

1 tablespoon (1¼) oil or melted
butter
2 egg whites

Sift the flour and salt into a mixing bowl and gradually work in the water and oil with a wooden spoon. Beat until smooth. Whisk the egg whites stiffly and fold them lightly and evenly into the batter. Use immediately.

106

FRITTER BATTER—2

4 servings:

5 oz. (1¼ cups) plain flour	**¼ pint (full ½ cup) light beer**
pinch of salt	**1 tablespoon (1¼) brandy**
2 egg yolks or 1 whole egg	

Make this richer batter well in advance and let it mature. Sift the flour and salt into a bowl, make a well in the centre and gradually beat in the egg yolks, beer and brandy with a wooden spoon, stirring until the batter is smooth and fairly thick.

ALMOND FRITTERS

My recipe is from the Greeks, who call the dish *scaltsounia* and make it usually with a dough rather than a batter. It is the sort of sweetmeat they delight to offer a visitor with coffee or a liqueur. Crushed peeled walnuts are sometimes used instead of almonds and the recipe can be varied indeed with any kind of nut or with a fruit filling.

4–6 servings:

8 oz. (2 cups) self-raising flour	**1 teaspoon (1¼) ground**
1 oz. (2 tablespoons) lard	**cinnamon**
milk to mix	**8 tablespoons (10) honey**
6 oz. (1 cup) ground almonds	**3 tablespoons (3¾) boiling water**
1 oz. (2 tablespoons) sugar	**1 teaspoon (1¼) rose water**

Make a dough with the flour, lard and enough milk to make it suitable for rolling out very thinly. Roll it out and cut it in 2-in. squares. Mix well the almonds, sugar and cinnamon. Put a little of the mixture on one square and cover it with another, wetting their edges and pressing them together to seal them. Deep fry in hot fat (about 375°F. or 191°C.) for 2 minutes. Drain them and then dip them in a mixture of the honey, water and rose water.

VIENNESE FRITTERS

Made in much the same way as the almond fritters are Viennese fritters, sometimes called brioche fritters because they are made with a yeast dough. They have fillings of cream, custard or chopped mixed fruits and are left in a warm place for half an hour to rise before cooking. Serve hot, dredged with sugar or dip them in a thin hot syrup (to taste) and serve them as soon as they are cold. In France Viennese fritters are also called Dauphine fritters, named after Marie Antoinette.

107

APPLE FRITTERS

4–6 servings:

4 ripe apples	**brandy**
sugar (to taste)	**fritter batter 1 or 2** (pages 106–7)
juice of ½ lemon or orange	

Core and peel the apples and cut them in rings ½ in. thick. Sprinkle them with sugar, lemon or orange juice and brandy to cover them. Let them stand for 20–30 minutes. Then with a skewer or a fork, dip the slices separately in the batter. Fry in deep fat at 370°F.–380°F. (188°C.–195°C.) until they are golden. Remove them from the pan, drain them on absorbent kitchen paper, dredge with fine sugar and serve them at once.

FRUIT FRITTERS

Fruit fritters, made in the same way as apple fritters, can include whole strawberries, raspberries or stoned cherries, stripped segments of oranges or tangerine or ¼-in.-thick pieces of pineapple.

BLOSSOM FRITTERS

Flower fritters are made with whole flowers or separated petals – of acacia, elder, violet, rose and other flowers. Stems of course are trimmed off. Sprinkle the blossoms with sugar and steep them in rum, brandy or liqueur for half an hour. Dip them in the batter and deep-fry them, by the spoonful. Drain and serve dredged with sugar.

SOUFFLÉ FRITTERS

Soufflé fritters are made with a choux paste (page 135). When they began back in the Middle Ages they were called *beignets venteux* or windy puffs. They are also known as nuns' sighs (*soupirs*) since some Frenchmen find the older *pets de nonne* too vulgar. I like Pomiane's description of them. Drop them into the hot fat and watch them swimming on the surface, he says. 'They swell and roll over and over like small porpoises'.

Divide the paste into walnut-size balls and drop them into moderately hot (350°F. or 177°C.) oil. If it is too hot the fritters will not puff up satisfactorily. Don't put in too many at a time, since the fritters should not touch each other. Raise the heat slightly to give them the golden finish. Strain and serve them sprinkled with icing (confectioners') sugar.

Oranges à la Turque (page 163) and Crystallized Flowers (page 152)
OVERLEAF *Vacherin Glacé aux Raisins Sec (page 150)*

Alternatively, after you have drained them you can make a small slit in the side and fill them, using a pastry forcing-bag, with fruit purée, jam or French pastry cream. Or you can serve them unfilled, with a jam sauce, honey sauce or zabaglione sauce.

WAFFLES

Waffles have been popular for at least 800 years and some of the ancient waffle irons are minor works of art, imprinting the waffles with coats of arms, religious symbols and other decorations. With today's irons cooking time varies but generally 2–3 minutes is sufficient. The iron should be hot before the batter goes in. It should not be overfilled – or the waffle will not rise properly. If the waffle tends to stick to the iron, cook it for a little longer. If waffles must be kept waiting, put them on a wire rack in a warm place. Stacking them turns them soggy.

Maple syrup is the usual accompaniment but warmed jam, zabaglione, syllabub or indeed any fairly thin sweet sauce goes well too. They can also be topped with whipped cream and strawberries, raspberries or loganberries.

4 servings:

4 oz. (1 cup) self-raising flour
pinch of salt
$\frac{1}{2}$ oz. (1 tablespoon) fine sugar
1 egg, separated

2 tablespoons ($2\frac{1}{2}$) melted butter
$\frac{1}{4}$ pint (full $\frac{1}{2}$ cup) milk

Mix the dry ingredients, add the egg yolk, melted butter and milk and beat with a wooden spoon until smooth. Whisk the egg white stiffly and fold it into the batter. Pour the batter thinly on to a well-greased hot iron, close it and cook until the waffle is golden-brown and crisp all over, which means turning the iron if it is non-electric. Serve at once. Optionally, $\frac{1}{2}$ teaspoon ($\frac{2}{3}$) mixed spice can be added to the dry ingredients.

BATTER PUDDINGS

Batter pudding in its simplest form is the English basic pancake batter (page 103) in a well-buttered baking tin (about 7 in. square) baked in a pre-heated fairly hot oven (400°F., mark 6) until it is well risen, about 45 minutes. Then cut it in sections and serve it with a jam sauce or treacle sauce. Chilled whipped cream or ice-cream goes well as a sauce too. The batter may include up to a teaspoonful of ground cinnamon or ground ginger.

Batter puddings can have a fruit base. For instance, peel, core and slice 1 lb. cooking apples and put them in the buttered baking dish. Sprinkle them with the grated rind of ½ lemon and 4 oz. (½ cup) sugar. Pour the batter over them and bake as for the plain pudding. Alternatively, use 1 lb. of very young rhubarb sweetened with soft brown sugar to taste.

CLAFOUTI AUX CERISES

Clafouti is a batter pudding that is a speciality of the gastronomically notable province of Limousin in France (now divided between the departments of Corrèze and Haute Vienne). It usually contains black cherries but can be made with other small fruits or with sliced apples, pears or peaches. The version here makes a rather special dish. In the batter you can substitute some of the marinade liquor from the cherries for a like quantity of the milk.

4–6 servings:

1 lb. sweet black cherries	**4 eggs**
4 oz. (½ cup) brandy	**3 oz. (full ⅓ cup) butter, melted**
4 oz. (1 cup) plain flour	**½ pint (1¼ cups) milk**
pinch of salt	
3 oz. (full ⅓ cup) vanilla-flavoured sugar	

Stone the cherries and steep them in the brandy for at least 2 hours. Sift the flour and to it add the salt and about half the sugar. Stir in the unbeaten eggs and 2 oz. (¼ cup) butter. Whisk in the milk gradually. Butter a flameproof oven-to-table dish, pour in some of the batter and cook it on top of the stove until it just begins to firm. Spread over this batter the drained cherries and nearly all the rest of the sugar, saving just enough to sprinkle on top later. Sprinkle a little of the marinating liquor on. Pour in evenly the rest of the batter. Cook in a moderate oven until the batter is well risen, about 45 minutes. Sprinkle with sugar before serving.

SWEET OMELETTES

Any omelette fancier can name or make her favourite sweet omelette and there is enormous scope for variations, particularly in the fillings and finishings. In chapter 3 there's a recipe for a baked soufflé omelette. More often, omelettes are cooked in a heavy-based pan on the top of the cooker and sometimes, though not always, flashed under the grill (broiler). Allow 1½ to 2 eggs per person, according to the size and richness of the accompaniments. A 6-in. pan is fine for single omelettes. An 8-in. pan can take 5 eggs and a 10-in. up to 8 eggs.

114

BASIC SWEET OMELETTE

2 servings:

4 eggs
½ oz. (1 tablespoon) sugar
pinch of salt

1 tablespoon (1¼) tepid water
or single (light) cream
butter for cooking

Beat well together the first four ingredients. Into a 6-in. omelette pan, put about ¼ oz. (1½ teaspoons) butter and heat it until the butter bubbles but is not brown. Pour in half the egg mixture and slightly reduce the heat. Lift the edges of the omelette with a spatula or palette knife and tilt the pan to run liquid from the centre under the edges. When the centre is creaming, fold the omelette at once in half and slip it on to a warm plate. Repeat the procedure for the second omelette.

OMELETTE FINISHINGS

With this basic sweet omelette, fillings or toppings or both are as interesting and as varied as they are with pancakes.

STRAWBERRY OMELETTE

Sliced strawberries, lightly sugared and softened over gentle heat, with blackcurrant liqueur, make a superb filling. Other soft fruits can be used similarly, with other liqueurs.

FLAMED RUM OMELETTE

Having made and folded the omelettes, set them in a silver or other flame-proof dish, sprinkle them with sugar and glaze them under a hot grill (broiler). Put 3 or 4 tablespoons (3¾–5) rum into a well-warmed punch ladle, set it alight, pour it over the glazed omelettes and carry them, flaming, to table. Brandy or kirsch can be used in the same way. As I've said (see *flaming*, pages 25–6) the residual flavour governs the choice of the spirit. Apart from that, flaming fried dishes serve the purpose of burning off any excess pan fat.

NORMANDY OMELETTE

A large omelette, to be suitably divided, is better than individual ones for this particular dish. Make the omelette (above) using cream as the liquid. To

115

prepare the filling for 4 servings, pare and core 2 cooking apples and slice them thickly. Cook them in butter with vanilla-flavoured sugar to taste. When they have softened, remove the pan from the heat and stir in 3 tablespoons ($3\frac{3}{4}$) of double (heavy) cream and then 3 tablespoons ($3\frac{3}{4}$) calvados. When the omelette is ready spread the filling on one half of it, fold it, sugar-glaze it under a hot grill. Put it on to a warm serving dish with, if you like, a ring of whipped cream added just before serving.

JAM OMELETTE

Make the omelettes in the usual way (page 115) and spread them with warmed jam before folding. Put them on a hot serving dish, sprinkle them well with sugar and, with a very hot skewer, sear the sugar in criss-cross pattern. Apricot jam seems to marry well with sweet omelettes. So do fruit compotes bound with a suitable jam and a flavouring of liqueur.

fruits, fruit sauces and nuts

Ever since Eve showed just how magic they can be, fresh-plucked from the tree, fruits have been a delight to man. Fruits and nuts come into innumerable sweets but we are concerned in this chapter with desserts that are quint-essentially of fruits or nuts and with fruit sauces, purées, juices and glazes. Strawberries, pineapples and rhubarb are included although, botanically speaking, they are not fruits at all.

FRESH FRUITS

The simplest of all desserts is a bowl of cool fresh fruits. Most of them reveal new qualities when eaten with cheese. Try, for instance, a slice of apple spread with Brie or topped with a slice of mature Cheddar. Soft fruits go happily with soured cream or cream cheeses. Again, there are infinite varia-tions in dusting soft fruits (or other fruits peeled and diced) with sugar and marinating them in lime, lemon, orange or apple juice or in dessert wines or liqueurs using 1–2 tablespoons ($1\frac{1}{4}$–$2\frac{1}{2}$) per serving of fruit. Combine the marinade liquor with whipped cream to serve with the fruit.

FROSTED FRUIT

As a dessert or a decoration, grapes, cherries and black, red or white currants can be sugar-frosted. Dip clusters of them in lightly whipped egg white and toss them in fine sugar. Dry them on a rack.

DRESSED FRESH FRUIT

Many fresh fruits can take on extra interest if they are dressed with toppings of creams, creamy mixtures or soft meringues or are caramelized with sugar. Take, for instance, peaches-and-cream caramel.

117

PEACHES-AND-CREAM CARAMEL

Ripe apricots and nectarines are equally delicious served this way.

4 servings:

4 peaches
1 oz. (2 tablespoons) fine sugar
3 tablespoons (3¾) curaçao

12 oz. (1½ cups) double
(heavy) cream
6–7 oz. (¾ cup) soft brown sugar

Blanch the peaches in boiling water for 2 or 3 minutes for easy peeling. Peel them, halve them carefully and cut the flesh into ½-in. slices. Lay them in a soufflé dish, sprinkle on the fine sugar and then the liqueur. Whip the cream until it is bulky and stiff enough to spread completely over the peach slices. Spread it and refrigerate for 3 hours. Spread the top with brown sugar to a depth of about ½ in. Put under a medium grill until the sugar caramelizes.

AMOR FRIO

Light and fresh to the palate, this Spanish dish befits its charming name which I translate as cool love. It is a good finisher after a *paella* or other rice dish. The sugar and the dryness of the sherry are adjustable. For me, in this recipe, the choice is an amontillado or a fino.

8 servings:

½ oz. (2 tablespoons) gelatine
4 oz. (½ cup) sugar
pinch of salt
good pinch of ground
   cinnamon
4 eggs, separated
¾ pint (scant 2 cups) milk

3 large oranges
3 tablespoons (3¾) sherry
1 tablespoon (1¼) lemon juice
¼ pint (full ½ cup) double
   (heavy) cream, whipped
1 oz. (3 tablespoons) blanched,
   chopped walnuts

In the top of a double saucepan, mix the gelatine, sugar, salt, cinnamon and egg yolks. Add the milk and cook the mixture over boiling water, stirring constantly, until it thickens. Turn it into a bowl and put it into the refrigerator until it is beginning to set. Grate the rind of one orange and reserve the zest. Meanwhile, peel the oranges, separate the segments and skin them. Cut the segments in half crosswise and put them in a bowl with the sherry. Put the bowl in the refrigerator. When the egg mixture begins to set, combine it with the lemon juice, two-thirds of the oranges, all the sherry, the whipped cream and the grated rind of 1 orange. Beat the egg whites until they are stiff and fold them into the mixture. Pile it into 8 individual glass dishes and sprinkle the tops with finely chopped nuts. Decorate with the remaining halved orange segments.

118

PASSION-FRUIT FLUMMERY

The Australians and New Zealanders make this fairy-light summery dessert with passion fruit sun-ripened on the vine (when it is surely one of the world's most wonderful fruits). The little pips are of course eaten with the pulp.

4 servings:

½ **pint (1¼ cups) milk**	1 **tablespoon (1¼) sherry**
4 **oz. (½ cup) sugar**	**pulp of 8 ripe passion fruit**
¼ **pint (full ½ cup) double (heavy) cream**	

Soak the gelatine in a little of the milk. Bring the rest of the milk to the boil, stir in the sugar and pour the mixture over the gelatine. Let it cool until it is almost setting. Whip the cream until it is stiff and whip in the sherry, the passion fruit and the gelatine mixture. Beat or blend it until smooth, pour it into a mould and chill it until set.

FRUIT SALADS

Among the hundreds of fruit salads, my preference is for the simplest – of fresh fruits only (perhaps with some additions of uncooked quick-frozen fruits) in their own marinade. The marinade can be incorporated in a sugar syrup – say, 2 oz. (¼ cup) sugar to ½ pint (1¼ cups) water for the sweetest fruits, 8 oz. (1 cup) sugar for the sharpest. Dissolve the sugar in the water, bring gently to the boil and boil for 5 minutes. Spices can be added during the boiling and 1–2 tablespoons (1¼–2½) lemon juice, liqueurs or spirits when the syrup cools. When I was in Jerez, visiting the great sherry family of Pedro Domecq, their dashing young export director, don Manuel Domecq Zurita, told me that their liqueur, Anis Domecq, was originally compounded by his grandmother to go in her fruit salads. It may sound unusual but, indeed, the aniseed liqueurs add quite a distinctive finish to many fruit salads.

Fruits which discolour quickly when peeled – apples, pears and bananas particularly – should go immediately into the cooled syrup or into cold water with lemon juice in it.

Salads of bottled fruits can include exotics like guavas, lychees, kumquats and figs. The syrups of these fruits or poached fruits can be sharpened with lemon juice or a 'dry' spirit like brandy, Calvados or vodka. There is included a marvellous salad-in-a-melon on page 161.

A dressy fruit salad is based on pineapple 'wheels' which can have whipped liqueur-enriched cream piped round each plate just before serving.

FRESH FRUIT WHEELS

4 servings:

10 oz. (2½ cups) strawberries	**fine sugar**
2 large oranges	**½ pint (1¼ cups) double**
4 slices fresh pineapple	**(heavy) cream**
4 tablespoons (¼ cup) Grand	
Marnier	

Reserving 4 large strawberries, cut the rest in halves. Peel the oranges, separate the segments and carefully skin each segment. Cut the segments in halves. Drain the pineapple slices and put one on each serving plate. Arrange halved orange segments, wheel fashion, on each pineapple slice and fill between and in the centre with halved strawberries. Top each centre with a whole strawberry. Sprinkle on a little liqueur – say ½ tablespoon on each. Sprinkle the strawberries with sugar to taste and leave in a cool place for 30 minutes. Whip the cream and then whip into it the rest of the liqueur. Just before serving, pipe cream around each plate.

FRESH MELON

Segmented cantaloups and honeydews or halved ogen and Charentais melons make wonderful desserts simply seeded, chilled and served with sugar or ground spice.

Stuffed melon. Halve the melon or melons and seed them. Scoop out the flesh and mix it in a fresh fruit salad. Thoroughly chill the melon shells and salad, mix in orange ice (page 95) and return the mixture to the melon shell to serve. One can also mix the melon flesh with a creamy sauce or a whip or with ice cream. Cored pineapple halves can be used similarly.

Melon with wine. Cut from the stem end of a large cantaloup a piece 2–3 in. across. Scoop out the seeds. Scoop out the flesh and dice it, sprinkle it generously with sugar and dessert wine, spirit or liqueur and return it to the melon shell. Replace the top piece, stand the melon in a bowl of crushed ice and leave it in the refrigerator for 2 hours. Replenish the ice and carry the bowl to table.

FRUIT PURÉES

Berry fruits and diced fruits of all kinds can be puréed raw in an electric blender and then put through a non-metallic fine sieve, with sugar added to taste. Without a blender, cooking the harder fruits (not berry fruits) softens them for sieving. Cook them in minimum water. For the thick purée needed for mousses, fools, chiffons and cream whips (chapter 6), strain off the juice before sieving.

RASPBERRY WHIP

Any fruit purée can be made into an attractive light dessert simply by whipping it with egg white. André Simon, for instance, recommended mashing a quart of ripe raspberries with plenty of sifted sugar. Sieve the mash, mix in 2 unbeaten egg whites and beat it to a stiff froth – to be chilled and served with whipped cream.

RØDGRØD MED FLØD (*Illustrated*)

Popular in Scandinavia are sweetened fruit purées thickened (with potato flour, cornflour, arrowroot or sago) and served as fruit soups or fruit 'creams'. The difference is that the soups incorporate enough water to stay liquid. The Danes' *rødgrød* (literally, red porridge), a 'cream' in this recipe, can be varied with blackcurrants, blackberries or strawberries.

4 servings:

½ **pint (1¼ cups) redcurrant purée**	**sugar to taste**
½ **pint (1¼ cups) raspberry purée**	**1 oz. (2 tablespoons) cornflour (cornstarch)**
	vanilla essence

Bring the mixed purées and sugar to the boil. Cream the cornflour with a little water, stir it into the purée with a little essence and boil gently for 2–3 minutes. Pour it into a serving dish or dishes and sprinkle it with sugar to prevent a skin forming as it cools. Decorate with sprigs of redcurrants and serve it with cream or a flavoured white sauce (page 64).

FRUIT JUICES

Fruit juices which cannot be squeezed or pressed from the fruit may be made by cooking fresh fruit. For 1 pint (2½ cups) juice, put 1 lb. fruit in 1 pint (2½ cups) water with sugar to taste. Bring it to the boil and simmer it for 5 minutes. Cool and strain it without breaking the fruit. For juices of strawberries, mulberries and the like, pour hot sugar syrup over the fruit. Juices can be thickened with arrowroot or cornflour for sauces (page 122), moulds (page 63) and glazes (page 122) or with gelatine for jellies (page 87).

ORANGE OR PINEAPPLE RICE

For a distinctive rice pudding, cook 2 oz. (⅓ cup) rice in 1 pint (1¼ cups) orange or pineapple juice and 1 oz. (2 tablespoons) sugar in a double saucepan over boiling water until the rice is tender, about 40 minutes. Cool it, whip ¼ pint (full ½ cup) double (heavy) cream and fold it into the rice.

FRUIT SAUCES AND GLAZES

Lemon and orange sauces are treated separately below. For the rest, to keep the true flavour, the fruits should be raw or, if heated, cooked as briefly as possible. For fruits which normally need to be well cooked, the jam-based sauce is the answer or the fruit cooked as a thin jam.

FRUIT SAUCES

Fruit sauces can be simple purées. Sugar and flavourings will be according to taste and the blandness or sharpness of the dessert the sauce accompanies. Flavourings can be spices, essence, citrus juice, spirits or liqueurs. For thicker sauces, cream 1 tablespoon (1¼) arrowroot with a little water and stir it into ¾ pint (scant 2 cups) boiling fruit juice or purée, stirring until it thickens.

JAM-BASED SAUCES

Jam and marmalade sauces are in chapter 2. They can be enriched by adding to the jam a like quantity of harmonizing jelly preserve – redcurrant or cranberry jelly with cherry jam, say, or quince jelly with apricot jam. They can also incorporate 2 tablespoons (2½) maraschino, drambuie, chartreuse or curaçao.

LEMON OR ORANGE SAUCE

Mix together ½ oz. (1 tablespoon) sugar with the finely grated rind of 1 large lemon (or orange). Melt ½ oz. (1 tablespoon) butter in a heavy-based pan over low heat. Stir in 1 tablespoon (1¼) cornflour (cornstarch) to make a roux and add ½ pint (1¼ cups) water, stirring until boiling. Add the juice of the lemon (or orange) to the sugar and stir it in, simmering for a few minutes. When it has cooled a little, stir in 2 well-beaten egg yolks. Gently reheat the sauce but do not let it boil. Serve it hot or cold and enriched, if you like, with curaçao.

FRUIT GLAZES

Fruit glazes can be potted like jam or used immediately. Boil 1 lb. (2 cups) sugar and ¼ pint (full ½ cup) water to 240°F., add 8 oz. (¾ cup) fruit purée, reboil to 230°F. and strain.

For another fruit glaze, melt 8 tablespoons (10) jam with 4 tablespoons (5) water and strain. To thicken this glaze, boil the strained liquid gently to the desired consistency or bring it to the boil and add 1 tablespoon (1¼) arrowroot creamed with water, stirring until the glaze is thick and clear.

POACHING FRUITS

The words stewed fruit conjure up, for me, a mess with the heart cooked out of it. Poaching, a method of keeping as much as possible of the original flavour, is done in a sugar syrup or in sweetened wine. The liquid can be reduced by boiling but the fruit itself should simmer only, not boil. Indeed strawberries, raspberries and the like do not go into the heating pan at all. The liquid is best poured over the berries some minutes after it has been removed from the heat – 'half-cooled' as Escoffier called it – and then covered until cold. Fresh pineapple which is to be used with gelatine should first be cooked. Simmer it in rings, peeled and cored, for 5 minutes in sugar syrup.

The poaching syrup can vary with the fruit. For flavour variations add vanilla or other essence and/or spices (chapter 1) or add strips of orange or lemon rind or the crushed kernels of stone fruits during the cooking and strain the syrup on to the fruit in the serving dish.

Poaching in wine. Firm fruits like cherries or cooking pears are good poached in claret or burgundy using ½ pint (1¼ cups) wine to 2 lb. fruit and 8 oz. (1 cup) sugar. Put all the ingredients in the pan, bring it gently to simmering point, cover and simmer for 5–6 minutes.

CONDÉ, HÉLÈNE, FLAMBÉ

Fruits *à la Condé* are poached in a vanilla-flavoured syrup, cooled and served on a creamed-rice mould (page 61). They are covered with a contrasting jam or purée, often laced with kirsch.

Pears (or other fruits) *Hélène* are poached in vanilla-flavoured syrup chilled and served on a base of vanilla ice cream (page 91). Chocolate sauce is served with them.

For flaming or flamed fruits (*flambé*) the poaching syrup is concentrated and sometimes mixed with a fruit purée before it is poured hot over the hot

123

poached fruit in a fireproof dish. A ladleful (say, 4–5 tablespoons) of warmed brandy, rum or other spirit is poured over and set aflame.

COMPOTES

Compotes can be of one fruit or mixed fruits, most often lightly poached. Prunes and other dried fruits should be soaked overnight in water or a half-and-half mixture of wine and water, then simmered in a syrup of the liquid and sugar – 2–4 oz. ($\frac{1}{4}$–$\frac{1}{2}$ cup) sugar to $\frac{1}{2}$ pint (1$\frac{1}{4}$ cups) liquid – for 5 minutes. The syrup can be flavoured with spices, essence or zest.

Berries, stoned cherries or quartered large fruits can be covered with sugar – say, 12 oz. (1$\frac{1}{2}$ cups) sugar to 1 lb. fruit – to make their own syrup and then cooked in a covered dish in a moderate oven for 10 minutes. Crushed fruit kernels in a muslin bag in the juice improve the flavour. Remove them before serving the fruit.

The word compote is also applied to fruits cooked for bottling but they are equally good sampled immediately, hot or cold. For instance, prick 1 lb. whole kumquats with a fork and simmer them until tender in sugar syrup, about 30 minutes. Optionally add 2 oz. ($\frac{1}{2}$ cup) finely chopped preserved ginger and the juice of $\frac{1}{2}$ lemon.

BRANDIED COMPOTES

Apricot, nectarine or peach halves, skinned and stoned, can be tightly packed with an equal weight of sugar into screw-top jars to make their own liquor. Fill the jars to the brim with the fruit and sugar and cover them loosely. Top up with brandy each day until all the sugar is dissolved and the jars are full. Seal the jars tightly and store in a cool dark place for 6 months.

A quicker way: make a syrup of $\frac{1}{2}$ lb. (1 cup) sugar for each 1 lb. fruit. Put the fruit and the cooled syrup into the jars and fill them to the brim with brandy. Seal the jars tightly and store in a cool dark place for 2 weeks.

CANDIED, CRYSTALLIZED, GLACÉ FRUIT

Candying fruit and peel belongs to preserving rather than to desserts. For crystallized fruit, skewer each piece of candied fruit, dip it quickly into boiling water and toss it in fine sugar. For glacé fruit dip the candied fruit in warm syrup made with 1 lb. (2 cups) sugar dissolved in $\frac{1}{4}$ pint (full $\frac{1}{2}$ cup) water. Boil 1 minute. For dipping, use a little syrup in a cup and renew it when it clouds. Dry the fruit on a rack.

124

SUMMER PUDDING

A summer pudding can be simply fruit juice thickened with cornflour (cornstarch) – 1½ oz. (3 tablespoons) cornflour to 1 pint (2½ cups) juice – and served with cream. The name however usually applies to the following type of sweet, made with sharp and colourful soft fruits – blackberries, raspberries, loganberries, and black and redcurrants.

4 servings:

4–5 slices white bread　　　　　**5 oz. (full ½ cup) sugar**
2 tablespoons (2½) water　　　　**1 lb. mixed redcurrants and**
　　　　　　　　　　　　　　　　raspberries

Slice the bread thinly (about ¼ in.), cut off the crusts and line a 1½-pint (1-quart) pudding basin with the slices, leaving no gaps. Stir the water and sugar together and bring to the boil. Add the fruits and simmer briefly until they are tender but still retain their shape. Pour them into the basin and cover them with slices of bread. Put a weighted saucer on top and leave the basin in a cold place overnight. Turn out the pudding and serve it with cream.

PEASANT GIRL WITH VEIL

Bondepige med Slør is the name of this dessert in Denmark where I first tasted it. It can be served hot as well as cold. A little raspberry jam or cranberry sauce can be mixed with the fruit.

4 servings:

8 oz. (5⅓ cups) fresh　　　　　**white sugar to taste**
　breadcrumbs　　　　　　　　**¼ pint (full ½ cup) cream,**
3 oz. (⅓ cup) brown sugar　　　　**whipped**
2 oz. (¼ cup) butter　　　　　　**2 oz. (2 squares) chocolate**
1½ lb. cooking apples

Mix the crumbs and brown sugar and fry them in minimum butter until crisp. Peel, core and slice the apples and bring them to the boil in minimum water with white sugar to taste. Cool and layer them alternately with crumbs in a glass serving dish, finishing with a layer of crumbs. Cool thoroughly, spread with cream and sprinkle with grated chocolate.

COLD FRUIT FLANS AND SAVARINS

For filling any of the flan cases in chapter 4 you need 1 lb. of the chosen fruit, 1 teaspoon (1¼) arrowroot and 2 oz. (¼ cup) sugar. Poach the fruit (page 123). Remove the fruit from the poaching liquid and thicken the liquid with the arrowroot. Boil gently for 10 minutes and cool. Arrange the fruit in the case, pour the cooled syrup over the fruit and chill. Serve it with cream.

Alternatively, half fill a baked sweet short pastry case (page 140) with French pastry cream (page 137). Arrange ½ lb. fresh sliced fruit or whole small fruits over the cream. Cover the fruit with a glaze and chill the flan. Sliced peaches go very well with an apricot glaze.

A syrup-soaked savarin (page 142) on a serving dish, filled with mixed fresh fruits, gives 8–10 servings. Finish with any flourish of decoration such as whipped cream, Chiboust or frangipane cream (pages 137, 144) patterned with angelica and chopped nuts. Alternatively, fill the centre with poached peach or pear halves on a bed of Chantilly or French pastry cream (page 139), topped with ½ pint (1¼ cups) apple sauce mixed with ¼ pint (full ½ cup) rum or liqueur.

PAVLOVA

The Pavlova is Australian, a meringue shell lined with whipped cream and filled with fruit – ideally, for me, diced eating apples blended with sun-ripened passion fruit. The case can be filled, as a variant, with ice cream or with a curd made with chopped pineapple and pineapple syrup.

4–6 servings:

4 egg whites	**½ teaspoon lemon juice**
8 oz. (1 cup) fine sugar	filling:
2 teaspoons (2½) cornflour	**½ pint (1¼ cups) double**
(cornstarch)	**(heavy) cream, whipped**
vanilla essence	**12 oz. (1½ cups) fruit flesh**

Draw an 8-in. circle on silicone (non-stick) paper and lay the paper on a baking sheet. Whisk the egg whites stiffly, beat in half the sugar and whisk stiff again. Add the rest of the sugar mixed with the cornflour and then fold in the vanilla essence and lemon juice. Spread the mixture on the paper to form an 8-in. bowl-shape shell. Bake it in the centre of a slow oven (300°F., mark 1) until firm and just coloured, 1½–2 hours. Cool it before carefully removing the paper. Put the shell on a flat cake tray, line it with the cream and fill it with the fruit.

MELON ALASKA

While the better known baked Alaska is featured on page 101, in the melon Alaska it's the melon that makes all the difference. The Charentais melon and the Ogen have a quite marvellous quality in fragrance and texture for this dessert, though a good honeydew or cantaloup will serve the purpose too. And if you have a golden papaya to hand, use it and count yourself blessed.

4 servings:

2 Charentais melons	**3 egg whites**
1-lb. block orange ice cream	**6 oz. (¾ cup) fine sugar**
3 dozen almonds	**4 tablespoons (5) curaçao**

Cut the melons in half, scoop out the seeds and put the halved fruits to chill. Freeze the ice cream until hard. Blanch and halve the almonds. When the ice cream is hard, whisk the egg whites with a little of the sugar and whisk in the rest of the sugar gradually until the meringue mixture can stand in stiff peaks. Put a quarter of the ice cream in each half-melon and pour over it a tablespoon of curaçao. Cover the filling and the exposed melon flesh with meringue, making sure that it extends right out to the melon rind to give a complete envelope to the filling and flesh. Stick halved almonds, porcupine fashion, in each mound of meringue. Bake in a very hot oven until meringue and almonds are tinged light brown, 3 or 4 minutes. Serve immediately.

BANANA FROST-AND-FIRE

It comes from the Carribbean and has one great disadvantage, at least for me, since it conjures up an almost unbearable nostalgia for those islands of beatitude. But I include it here, too, as much for its name as for the subtle delights of its flavours. As a variant, equally good, one can substitute sun-ripened fresh pineapple for the bananas and use rum-flavoured ice-cream.

4 servings:

1-lb. block coffee ice cream	**3 bananas**
3 egg whites	**2 tablespoons (1½) rum**
1 oz. (2 tablespoons) fine sugar	

Freeze the ice cream until very hard. Stiffly beat the egg whites, gradually beating in the sugar to make a soft meringue. Peel the bananas, halve them lengthways and cut the halves into three. Put half the banana pieces in a shallow oblong ovenproof dish slightly larger than the block of ice cream. Put the block on the base of banana, surround and cover it with the remaining banana slices. Swirl the meringue mixture over all, spreading it right to the edge of the dish all round to seal in the ice cream. Put the dish into a very

127

hot oven and bake until the meringue is just beginning to colour, about 3 or 4 minutes. Meanwhile, warm the rum in a ladle. Take the dish from oven to table, pour the rum over it, ignite it and serve while still flaming.

BAKING FRUITS

For cooked fruits that are fruitier, simply put the fruit in an oven dish with about 2 oz. ($\frac{1}{4}$ cup) sugar to 1 lb. fruit and bake it in a moderate oven (350°F., mark 4) for 20 minutes. Berries and black cherries are wonderful this way. With halved pears, apples, peaches or apricots one can put them in the dish, cut side up, fill the core hollow with orange juice and pour 2 tablespoons of honey or maple syrup on each half. Also, one might fill the hollows with sugar and pour 2 tablespoons ($2\frac{1}{2}$) red wine on each half.

BAKED STUFFED PEACHES

Variations are numerous in this Italian dish. The filling can be enriched with liqueur or with a little finely chopped candied peel. The peach halves can be baked 'open' (that is, cut side up) with the filling, bound with an egg yolk and 1 oz. (2 tablespoons) butter, in a smooth mound covering them. Or bake them cut side down on rounds of sponge cake which have been coated in hot sieved jam and rolled in chopped almonds.

4 servings:

4 ripe peaches	**2 oz. ($\frac{1}{3}$ cup) almonds, pounded**
2 oz. ($\frac{1}{2}$ cup) crushed ratafia biscuits	**2 oz. ($\frac{1}{4}$ cup) sugar**
	4 tablespoons (5) white wine

Blanch, skin, halve and stone the peaches. Scoop out some of the flesh and mix it with the ratafias, the almonds and half the sugar. Put this filling in the peach halves, fit the halves together and put them in an oven dish. Dissolve the rest of the sugar in the wine and pour it over the peaches. Cook them in a moderate oven (350°F., mark 4) for 10 minutes and serve hot or cold.

BAKED APPLES

The Germans bake peeled and cored apples, stuffed with red jam and sunk in a custard mixture with stiffly-whisked egg whites folded into it. In a moderate oven (350°F., mark 4), the apples cook in 30–40 minutes. Quinces are good this way too.

In Britain apples have been baked in their skins for at least 600 years and

128

probably much longer. They are most simply cored and stuffed with brown sugar, topped with a knob of butter and set in an oven dish in water $\frac{1}{4}$ in. deep. Then they bake in the centre of a fairly hot oven (400°F., mark 6) for about 45 minutes.

You can ring changes by stuffing them with mincemeat or chopped dried fruits or candied fruits and peels, chopped nuts bound with cranberry or blueberry jelly. Or, 10–15 minutes before they finish cooking, cover the apples with sweetened meringue or top each with a marshmallow and return them to the oven.

BAKED BANANAS

Bananas can be baked simply covered with a sugar syrup with the juice of a lime or orange added for about 30 minutes in a slow oven (300°F., mark 1). Serve them with warm rum poured on and flamed. The Danes make them the basis of a baked fruit salad.

JAMAICAN BAKED BANANAS

Many of the English like their bananas not fully ripe, the flesh still firm and the skin only palely yellow. The Jamaicans pick such bananas for baking in their skins, this way:

6 servings:
$\frac{1}{2}$ pint (1$\frac{1}{4}$ cups) double (heavy) cream
4 tablespoons (5) rum

6 large bananas
sugar

Whip the cream, adding the rum as you whip. Split each banana lengthways and carefully remove the flesh without damaging the skin. Mash the flesh and blend it with the cream-rum mixture and sugar to taste. Pack it back into the skins. Put them, filling-side uppermost, on a baking tray and bake them in a fairly hot oven (400°F., mark 6) for 5 to 8 minutes. Serve immediately.

BAKED PINEAPPLE

Cut the top off a large pineapple and scoop out the flesh without puncturing the skin. Discarding the core, dice the flesh and add the diced flesh of a ripe peach and sugar to taste. Soak the fruit in rum or brandy for 2 hours, put it into the pineapple shell, replace the top of the pineapple and bake it in a moderate oven (350°F., mark 4) for 30 minutes. At table one can pour over

129

the fruit mixture still in its shell a little warm rum or brandy – say, 4 table-spoons (5) – and set it alight.

BAKED FRUIT SALAD

6–8 servings:

¼ lb. pitted prunes	1 oz. (scant ¼ cup) raisins
¼ lb. dried apricots	3 tablespoons (3¾) honey
1½ oz. (3 tablespoons) butter	½ pint (1¼ cups) orange juice
4 bananas	grated rind 1 orange

Soak the prunes and apricots overnight in water (or white wine). Drain them and chop them coarsely. Butter a shallow oven dish with some of the butter. Quarter the bananas lengthways and arrange them in the dish. Sprinkle over them the raisins, prunes and apricots. Mix the honey well with the orange juice and rind and pour it over the fruit. Dot with the remaining butter and bake in a moderate oven (350°F., mark 4) for 30 minutes.

NUTS

All kinds of nuts enrich our desserts. Here are recipes where the nuts are the essence of the dish. First among them are the macaroon mixtures. Besides almonds, they are made from the kernels of cherries, peaches and apricots and from coconut. The mixtures make good fillings for tartlets and flans. Biscuits made from them can be crushed to add distinctive flavour and texture in many cold sweets, as our earlier recipes have shown. The biscuits are also called ratafias and, in Italy, *amaretti*.

SARD AMARETTI

In Italy's wonderful island of Sardinia there are Sardinians who have never been to the coast, let alone the mainland. These are the proud mountain people of the Genargentu – a whole world away from the Costa Smeralda and other tourist resorts. It was in one of the mountain villages I found my recipe for the best macaroons I have ever tasted, though the recipe is adapted since there were no electric blenders in those parts when its magic was first compounded. It is the subtle combination of bitter and sweet almonds that makes them so special.

Eat them straight away – some of them, anyway. Strong-minded people will like to know they keep for a week or so in an airtight tin. They can be the

130

crisp, contrasting flourish to serve with smooth ice creams and other cold desserts. Use them, if you're a perfectionist, for the strawberry amaretti too.

for 16 macaroons:

2 oz. ($\frac{1}{3}$ cup) bitter almonds	**8 oz. (1 cup) fine sugar**
6 oz. (1 cup) sweet almonds	**rice paper**
2 egg whites	**icing (confectioners') sugar**

Blanch the almonds in boiling water, plunge them in cold water and peel off their skins. Dry them, without browning them, on a baking sheet in a warm oven. Blend them to a powder in an electric blender or with a pestle and mortar. Beat the egg whites until peaky but not dry and fold in the almonds and fine sugar. Lay a sheet of rice paper on a baking sheet and pipe the mixture on to it in rounds of about 1-in. diameter. Leave to settle for about 3 hours and bake in a moderate oven. They take about 15 minutes, by which time they should be just tinged brown. Cool them on a wire rack and then trim off any excess rice paper. Sprinkle with icing sugar.

STRAWBERRY AMARETTI

4 servings:

16 macaroons	**icing (confectioners') sugar**
$\frac{1}{2}$ lb. strawberries	**$\frac{1}{4}$ pint (full $\frac{1}{2}$ cup) double**
2 tablespoons ($2\frac{1}{2}$) medium	**(heavy) cream**
sherry or madeira	**$\frac{1}{4}$ pint (full $\frac{1}{2}$ cup) single (light)**
2 tablespoons ($2\frac{1}{2}$) orange juice	**cream**

Make the macaroons (Sard amaretti, above) or buy a 3-oz. packet. Reserving 4 large strawberries, slice the rest. Reserve 4 macaroons and lay the rest in 4 glasses of the wide squat type. Mix the wine with the orange juice and sprinkle it on the macaroons in the glasses. Put sliced strawberries into each glass with a sprinkling of icing sugar to taste. Whip all the cream together until it just holds its shape. Spoon most of it over the strawberries, saving enough to pipe a bit in the centre of each glass to mount a whole strawberry. Mount the strawberries. Chill for about 30 minutes and stick a macaroon in each glass before serving.

PECAN PIE

Americans can claim a certain expertise about pies, and pecan pie is a favourite. Since many of them tend to minimize their intake of animal fats, this recipe uses a pastry made basically from vegetable fat. The filling is very sweet which is why there is no sugar in the pastry or in the whipped cream which makes a good accompaniment. To cut preparation chores you can buy the pecans shelled, ready to use.

6 servings:

4 oz. ($\frac{1}{2}$ cup) white blended vegetable fat
1 oz. (2 tablespoons) butter
6 oz. (1$\frac{1}{2}$ cups) plain flour
pinch salt
3 tablespoons (3$\frac{3}{4}$) cold water
for the filling:
3 eggs

1 tablespoon (1$\frac{1}{4}$) milk
6 oz. ($\frac{3}{4}$ cup) demerara sugar
6 oz. ($\frac{3}{4}$ cup) maple or corn syrup
2 oz. ($\frac{1}{4}$ cup) softened butter
$\frac{1}{2}$ teaspoon ($\frac{2}{3}$) vanilla essence
6 oz. (1 cup) halved pecans

Cream together the white fat and the butter. Gradually stir in the sifted flour and salt, creaming well after each addition. Mix in the water thoroughly. Knead lightly with extra flour as this pastry is sticky to handle. Chill the pastry, roll it out and line a 9-in. oven-proof glass dish, fluting the edge. Put the dish to chill again while preparing the filling.

Beat the eggs and milk together. Boil the sugar and syrup together in a saucepan for 3 minutes. Stirring well, slowly pour the sugar-syrup on to the beaten eggs and stir in the butter and essence. Use half the nuts to cover the base of the pastry case. Spoon the syrup mixture over them and cover it with the remaining nuts. Bake in a hot oven (425°F., mark 7) for 10 minutes. Reduce the heat to 325°F. (mark 3) until the filling is set, a further 45 minutes. Serve the pie warm or cold with unsweetened whipped cream.

FYRSTEKAKE

This rich Norwegian almond pie is traditionally served cold but it is delicious warm too. Its name translates as Prince's Cake and you can add another princely touch by lacing the accompanying whipped cream with aquavit.

6 servings:
1 flan pastry recipe (page 47)
for the filling:
4 oz. ($\frac{2}{3}$ cup) ground almonds
4 oz. (scant cup) icing (confectioners') sugar, sifted

2 egg yolks
1 egg white
almond essence

Make the pastry and chill it. Grease an 8-in. straight-sided tin, a deep one, and line it with the pastry. Prick the base and flute the edges. Knead the cut-offs of pastry together, roll it out thinly and cut it into narrow strips. Put the tin and strips to chill while preparing the filling. Blend the almonds, sugar, egg yolks and a few drops of almond essence together. Whisk the egg white until it is stiff and fold in the mixture. Turn it into the pastry-lined tin and lattice the top with pastry strips. Bake in a hot oven (425°F., mark 7) for 15 minutes and then reduce the heat to 300°F. (mark 2) for about 30 minutes more. Serve in wedges with whipped cream.

CHESTNUTS

Chestnuts come from the Spanish or sweet chestnut tree not to be confused with childhood playthings called conkers which come from the horse chestnut tree. Conkers are strictly inedible. As we've seen (notably in the Nesselrode and the chestnut puddings in chapter 6) the sweet chestnut makes a wonderful contribution to our desserts. They can be roasted in front of the fire or in a special chestnut roaster or a hot oven. Serve them with fine sugar or with salt. Or, boiled until tender, they can be ground to a flour to make cakes or sieved to make macaroons. Glazed chestnuts, which the French call *marrons glacés*, are preserves which require so much time and patience that they are usually bought.

COMPOTE OF CHESTNUTS

A good Spanish way with chestnuts: take 1 lb. chestnuts, split the shells at the sharper end, boil them in water for 10 minutes, peel them and then take off their skins. Dissolve 6 oz. ($\frac{3}{4}$ cup) sugar in $\frac{1}{2}$ pint ($1\frac{1}{4}$ cups) water, add the chestnuts, cover and simmer until the chestnuts are tender, about 1 hour. Cool the compote, add 2 tablespoons ($2\frac{1}{2}$) Maraschino and chill.

COFFEE CHESTNUT

4 servings:

1 lb. sweet chestnuts	**$\frac{1}{4}$ pint (full $\frac{1}{2}$ cup) very strong**
2 oz. ($\frac{1}{4}$ cup) sugar	**black coffee**
2 egg yolks	**3 tablespoons ($3\frac{3}{4}$) rum**

Score the chestnuts at the pointed end, boil them for 10 minutes, peel and skin them. Simmer them with half the sugar and enough water to cover, until they are soft, about 1 hour. In a bowl over hot water (or in a double sauce-pan), mix together the egg yolks, the rest of the sugar, the coffee and the rum, stirring until the mixture thickens. Pour it over the strained chestnuts in a warmed serving dish.

133

pastries and gâteaux

The pastries that make some of our most glamorous desserts are rich in legends. The rum baba as we know it began apparently in the eighteenth century when Poland's King Stanislas discovered that kugelhupf tasted better sprinkled with rum and renamed it, after his favourite fictional hero, Ali Baba. He also liked to set it aflame as we do our Christmas puddings. When Stanislas married off his daughter to France's King Louis XV the cake moved west and became popular, first with a sauce of sweetened spiced Malaga wine. The beautiful Marie Antoinette, who married the luckless Louis XVI, took to Paris the Austrian passion for sweets made with yeast dough. They were soon the rage of the royal court. The same dough was used by a nineteenth-century Paris pastry-cook to evolve the Brillat-Savarin, named after the great gastronome who died in 1826. The names were shortened to baba and savarin in the series of resurgences of French pastry-making which began with Carême and his contemporaries around the beginning of the nineteenth century.

Choux pastry or *pâte à chou* – although developed in 1540 by a chef to France's Queen Catherine – got its present name in Carême's time. It was then too that pastry bags or forcing bags, almost always used to shape choux pastry nowadays, first made their appearance. The pundits argue about the origin of puff pastry but most of the argument seems irrelevant since cooks in England were making it in the Middle Ages and there is even evidence which suggests it was known to the ancient Greeks.

CHOUX PASTRY

Many air-light desserts are of choux pastry, also called cream-puff pastry. The golden rule is that it is always well cooked, firm and crisp. It makes choux buns or cream puffs, profiteroles, éclairs and gâteau St Honoré. The

134

buns can be filled with a variety of creams, salpicons of fruits, purées of *marrons glacés* or other nuts, jams and so on. They can be coated with chocolate or coffee icings or with caramelized sugar and built into a pyramid as a *croquembouche* with a spun sugar halo.

BASIC CHOUX PASTE

4 oz. ($\frac{1}{2}$ cup) butter
$\frac{1}{2}$ pint (1$\frac{1}{4}$ cups) water

5 oz. (1$\frac{1}{4}$ cups) plain flour
4 eggs

Heat the butter and water together in a pan and bring to the boil. Remove immediately from the heat and quickly sift in all the flour, stirring with a wooden spoon. Beat until the mixture forms into a ball of dough, cleanly leaving the sides of the pan. Add the eggs one by one, beating until the mixture is smooth and glossy and will just hold its shape when piped. Add any desired flavouring, such as vanilla, at this stage. Cool slightly before piping the paste on to wet baking sheets. Bake according to individual recipes.

PROFITEROLES

4 servings:
$\frac{1}{2}$ basic choux paste recipe
(above)
$\frac{1}{2}$ pint (1$\frac{1}{4}$ cups) double (heavy) cream

1 chocolate cream sauce recipe
(page 136)

Using a plain $\frac{1}{2}$-in. nozzle in the forcing bag, pipe the paste in walnut-size dollops on to greased baking sheets, leaving space for them to swell. Brush them with beaten egg. Bake in a pre-heated fairly hot oven (400°F., mark 6) for about 30 minutes, when the buns should be well risen, golden brown and firm. Cool them on a wire rack. Make a hole or slit in the side of each bun and pipe in the cream, lightly whipped if it is too 'wet'. Arrange the profiteroles on a serving dish and coat them with chocolate sauce. Alternatively, dust the buns with icing sugar and serve the sauce separately. As a variant, use any cream or custard filling.

CREAM PUFFS

These are made in the same ways as profiteroles but are steam-baked so that they puff up more. For 6 large puffs use $\frac{1}{2}$ basic choux paste recipe (above). Pipe it in six rounds, well-spaced, on a buttered baking sheet. Cover the baking sheet with an inverted deep tin (a roasting dish, for instance) and bake in a fairly hot oven (375°F., mark 5) for 45–50 minutes without lifting the tin. Remove the puffs carefully to cool on a wire rack. Pipe in a filling of puréed chestnuts mixed with twice their volume of whipped cream and a little kirsch.

CHOCOLATE CREAM SAUCE

½ lb. plain block chocolate
4 tablespoons (5) golden syrup (corn syrup)

¼ pint (full ½ cup) single (light) cream

This makes about ¾ pint (scant 2 cups). Put the broken chocolate into a saucepan and melt it over very low heat. Add the syrup and stir until thoroughly blended. Remove the pan from the heat and slowly add the cream, stirring. Serve warm. It is very good with ice cream as well.

GÂTEAU ST HONORÉ

There seems to be no gastronomic evidence why Honoré, a seventh-century bishop of Amiens, should be regarded as patron saint of pastrycooks – but he is and this rich dessert is named after him.

4 servings:

⅔ flan pastry recipe (page 47)
1 egg, beaten
½ basic choux paste recipe (page 135)
¼ pint (full ½ cup) double (heavy) cream
1½ oz. (3 tablespoons) fine sugar

3 tablespoons (3¾) water
1 recipe Chiboust cream or French pastry cream (page 137)
angelica and glacé cherries, for decoration

Roll the flan pastry into a 7-in. round, prick well and put it on a lightly greased baking tray. Brush round the edge with beaten egg. With about half the choux paste pipe a circle round the edge of the pastry and brush it with egg. Bake in the centre of a fairly hot oven (375°F., mark 5) for 20–30 minutes. Pipe the remaining choux paste into about 20 little walnut-sized balls on a separate buttered baking sheet, brush them with beaten egg and bake in the oven for the last 15 minutes. Cool the base and buns on a wire rack. Whip the cream lightly and pipe it into the buns. Dissolve the sugar in the water and boil until the syrup begins to take on a straw colour. With tongs or a skewer dip the buns in the syrup and stick them on to the choux pastry border of the base. Fill the centre of the gâteau with the Chiboust cream and decorate it with angelica and cherries. Optionally, quickly roll the syrup-coated buns in chopped pistachio nuts before sticking them on the border.

136

CHIBOUST CREAM

Chiboust cream, named after a nineteenth-century Parisian pastrycook, was René Roussin's choice when he served gâteau St Honoré with strawberries in maraschino to King George VI at Buckingham Palace. Some recipes, like Roussin's, incorporate gelatine with the egg whites. Optionally, flavour the cream with a liqueur added as it cools instead of vanilla. It is sometimes called St Honoré cream.

2 egg yolks
2 oz. (¼ cup) fine sugar
½ oz. (2 tablespoons) plain flour
½ vanilla pod
3 egg whites

½ oz. (1 tablespoon) cornflour (cornstarch)
½ pint (1¼ cups) milk

Cream the egg yolks with the sugar until pale, add the flours blended with a little of the milk and mix in well. Heat the rest of the milk with the vanilla pod almost to boiling point and remove the pod. Pour it on to the egg mixture, stirring well. Return it to low heat, stirring continuously until the mixture boils. Remove from the heat and immediately fold in the stiffly beaten egg whites. Leave to cool.

FRENCH PASTRY CREAM

French pastry cream is also called confectioner's custard and *crème patissière*.

4 egg yolks
3 oz. (full ⅓ cup) fine sugar

1 oz. (¼ cup) flour, sifted
½ pint (1¼ cups) vanilla-flavoured milk

Beat the yolks and sugar together until thick and pale. Beat in the flour, adding a little milk to form a paste. Heat the rest of the milk almost to boiling point and pour it on to the egg mixture stirring all the time. Return the mixture to the pan, stir over low heat until it boils and, stirring all the time, continue cooking until it is thick. Remove from the heat, strain and, stirring it from time to time, cool and then chill it.

PUFF PASTRY

The aristocrat of flaky pastries or *pâtes feuilletées*, puff pastry takes something over two hours to prepare but the melting luscious delights it makes to grace the end-of-dinner table are worth the effort. Much of the time is taken up in cooling the paste after each 'turn' so that the butter and flour are kept in the

137

separate layers in which the rolling and folding have arranged them. It is on this that the lightness of your pastry depends. For the same reason, after the last chilling the paste should be shaped and go into the preheated oven as quickly as possible. If any filling is to go into the paste before cooking, have it ready in advance so that the final shaping takes the minimum time. In view of the long preparation some cooks make twice as much paste as they need and use half of it later. It keeps, wrapped, in the refrigerator for several days.

BASIC PUFF PASTE

8 oz. (2 cups) plain flour
1 level teaspoon (1¼) salt
squeeze lemon juice

8 oz. (1 cup) unsalted butter
¼ pint (full ½ cup) iced water

Sift the flour and salt into a mixing bowl. Add the lemon juice and rub in a quarter of the butter, diced or flaked, as for short crust. Moisten with sufficient water to make a rather stiff dough. Turn it on to a lightly-floured board or slab and knead lightly until smooth and free from cracks. Roll it out into an oblong. Roll out the butter, which should be firm but not hard, into a flat cake and put it in the centre of the dough. Fold each edge of the dough into the centre, envelope fashion, press the edges together and roll the dough into a long narrow strip, taking care that the butter does not come through. Fold into three, wrap in greaseproof paper and leave in the refrigerator (not the coldest part) for 40 minutes. This is called one 'turn'. The rolling and folding process needs to be done seven times in all, with a rest in the refrigerator for at least 15 minutes after each 'turn'. Preheat the oven to the degree indicated in the recipe.

LARGE MILLE – FEUILLE

Preheat the oven to very hot (450°F., mark 8). For 6–8 servings use 1 basic puff paste recipe (above) and roll the paste out quite thinly, not more than ¼ in. This is easier to do between sheets of waxed or silicone paper. Cut the pastry into three or four 6-in. circles. Put these rounds on wet baking sheets, prick them with a fork, dredge with sugar and bake near the top of the oven until crisp and golden, 8–10 minutes. Finish one round for topping (see below) and, just before serving, sandwich the rounds together with fillings.

Topping variations. Spread the top round with a smooth layer of meringue, sprinkle it with sugar and put it back in the oven for a few minutes to set the meringue. Garnish the meringue with chopped nuts, glacé fruits or piped whipped cream, give the top round a coating of glacé icing (page 140) or

138

simply dust it with cinnamon-flavoured fine sugar or icing (confectioners') sugar.

Filling variations. Thick Chantilly cream, which is simply sweetened cream whipped and flavoured with liqueur, vanilla or other flavouring, may be used alone or combined with one third of its volume of sieved fruit purée. Alternatively, use French pastry cream (page 137), alone or blended with finely-chopped preserved ginger or candied fruits or peels.

GÂTEAU PITHIVIERS

6 servings:

1 basic puff paste recipe
 (page 138)
for the filling:
6 oz. (1 cup) ground almonds
2 eggs, beaten

4 oz. ($\frac{1}{2}$ cup) fine sugar
2 oz. ($\frac{1}{4}$ cup) butter
2 tablespoons (2$\frac{1}{2}$) rum
for the glaze:
$\frac{1}{2}$ **oz. (1 tablespoon) fine sugar**

Have the puff paste ready in the refrigerator. Preheat the oven to hot (425°F., mark 7). For the filling of almond cream, mix the almonds with one egg to a fine paste and add the sugar and flaked butter, blending together with a wooden spoon until quite smooth. Blend in nearly all the rest of the egg and then the rum until the paste is of a smooth spreading consistency. Roll out the pastry thinly to two rounds of about 8-in. diameter and trim them to fit exactly. Put one round on a wet baking sheet. Spread it with the almond filling to within about $\frac{3}{4}$ in. of the edge. Moisten the edge of the pastry with lukewarm water and cover with the second round. Press well all round the edge to seal the two rounds together. Brush with beaten egg. Rest for 5 minutes and then with the point of a knife mark the top with lines to form a lattice or rosette design. Bake for 25–30 minutes. A couple of minutes before the end of cooking time, sprinkle the gâteau with fine sugar to glaze at the top of the oven.

VOL-AU-VENT

Preheat the oven to very hot (450°F., mark 8). For 6–8 servings use 1 basic puff paste recipe rolled out about 1 in. thick. Put it, upside down, on a buttered baking sheet, and, with a sharp knife dipped in hot water, cut it in a circle, putting aside the trimmings. Cut to half the depth of the pastry another circle $\frac{3}{4}$ in. in from the edge. Brush the top with beaten egg and bake towards the top of the oven for 30–35 minutes, covering the pastry with greaseproof paper when it is brown. Remove the lid (the inner circle) with a knife, scoop out any soft pastry and dry out in the oven for 5–10 minutes more. Serve cold filled with whipped cream and soft fruit.

139

SWEET SHORT PASTRY

Many delicious cold dessert flans and tartlets are made with a sweet short pastry that has the advantage of keeping its shape (neither shrinking much nor spreading), can be rolled very thinly, has a crisp yet melting texture. The dough needs to rest for an hour and is even easier to handle if you make it a day ahead, put it in a plastic bag and keep it in a cool place. The basic recipe makes enough to line an 8-in. loose-bottomed tart ring or 6 shallow patty tins of 4½-in. diameter or 18 little 'boat' tins.

BASIC SWEET SHORT PASTE

2 oz. (¼ cup) butter	2 oz. (¼ cup) fine sugar
4 oz. (1 cup) plain flour	2 egg yolks
pinch of salt	

See that the butter is at room temperature. Sift the flour and salt together on a pastry board or marble slab. Make a well in the centre and add the sugar, flaked butter and egg yolks. Work these ingredients together with the finger-tips until well blended. Gradually work in the flour, knead lightly until smooth and leave the paste in a cool place for at least an hour. Preheat the oven to fairly hot (375°F., mark 5). Roll the paste out thinly, line the tart ring or patty tins and press lightly into shape. Bake in the centre of the oven until just coloured (5–7 minutes for 'boats', 15–20 minutes for the patties or the tart ring). Cool on a wire rack and fill with glazed fruits or a creamy filling or nut honey butter (below). The filling can, optionally, be covered with a glacé icing (below).

NUT HONEY BUTTER

12 oz. (1½ cups) butter	3 tablespoons (3¾) thick honey
12 oz. (1½ cups) fine sugar	2 tablespoons (2½) coffee
12 oz. (2 cups) nuts, ground	essence

To fill an 8-in. tart ring or 1½ dozen boats of cooked sweet short pastry. Cream the butter and sugar together until fluffy, beat in the nuts (pecans, filberts, walnuts or almonds), honey and essence. Pile into the pastry case or cases in smoothed mounds and chill until firm. Optionally top with coffee glacé icing (page 141).

GLACÉ ICING

To cover the top of an 8-in. tart and allow additional decoration or to cover a 6–8 in. cake all over. Sift 8 oz. (scant 2 cups) icing (confectioners') sugar into a pan and if the sugar is not already flavoured, add a few drops of flavouring essence. Add gradually 3 tablespoons (3¾) water over very gentle heat, stirring until it is warm only (too much heat will spoil it) and thick enough to coat the back of the spoon. Pour on to the centre of the tart ensuring a smooth flow all over. If piped whirls are wanted as decoration, add icing sugar to the icing to give piping consistency.

Coffee glacé icing
Replace 2 teaspoons (2½) of the water with coffee essence, using unflavoured sugar.

Fruit glacé icing
Replace some or all of the water with strained orange or other fruit juice, using unflavoured sugar.

Chocolate glacé icing
Melt 2 oz. (2 squares) grated chocolate in the water, boil for 2 minutes, cool and add sugar and flavouring.

YEAST DOUGH

Rich but light, savarins and babas are based on yeast dough, the variations coming in the fruity, creamy and liquorous additions. Served with syrup only, the basic paste recipe here makes enough for 8 individual babas or 8 servings of a savarin or large baba. They are usually served cold though they can be hot desserts too.

BASIC SAVARIN PASTE

1 teaspoon (1¼) sugar	**½ teaspoon (⅔) salt**
¼ pint (full ½ cup) milk	**4 eggs, beaten**
¼ oz. (1 tablespoon) dried yeast	**4 oz. (½ cup) butter**
8 oz. (2 cups) plain flour	

Dissolve the sugar in the milk warmed to 110°F. (43°C), sprinkle the yeast on top and leave it in a warm place until frothy – about 10 minutes. Put the slightly warmed sieved flour into a large bowl with the salt. Make a well in the centre and add the yeast mixture. Add the beaten eggs and beat the paste vigorously by hand to form a smooth dough, continuing the beating until the dough comes away from the sides of the bowl. Distribute flakes of softened butter evenly over the dough. Cover the dough and keep it in a

141

warm place until it has doubled its bulk – about $\frac{1}{2}$–$\frac{3}{4}$ hour. Knead the paste again before using so that the butter is absorbed.

SAVARIN (*Illustrated*)

Put the dough in a buttered ring mould, known as a savarin mould, filling it not more than three-quarters full. Leave it in a warm place until the dough has risen to the top of the mould, about 45 minutes. Meanwhile, preheat the oven to fairly hot (400°F., mark 6). Bake the savarin just above the centre of the oven for 10 minutes, reduce the heat to moderate (350°F., mark 4) and cook until rich brown, 30–35 minutes more. Allow to cool slightly before turning out of the mould. Soak it in your chosen syrup (below) and pile the centre with fruit (chapter 9) or other filling.

SAVARIN À LA CREME

For 8–10 servings, use 1 basic savarin paste recipe. After soaking the savarin in syrup, put it on a serving dish and fill the centre with 1 pint (2$\frac{1}{2}$ cups) thick French pastry cream (page 137) mixed with 2–3 oz. (about 1 cup) crushed macaroons. When this sweet is served hot it is liberally sprinkled with icing (confectioners') sugar which is then scorch-marked with a very hot skewer.

BABAS

For 8 individual babas use 1 basic savarin paste recipe (page 141) in which you can, optionally, incorporate 4 oz. ($\frac{2}{3}$ cup) currants or sultanas and grated zest of 1 lemon. Half fill the individual moulds and leave the dough to rise to the top. Bake near the top of a hot oven for 15–20 minutes. Turn out and soak with rum syrup or savarin syrup (below). When cold, the babas can be split and filled with cream and decorated with angelica, maraschino cherries or pistachio nuts.

SAVARIN SYRUP

$\frac{3}{4}$ **pint (scant 2 cups) water**	**1 sliced lemon**
$\frac{3}{4}$ **lb. (1$\frac{1}{2}$ cups) sugar**	$\frac{1}{2}$ **cinnamon stick**
1 sliced orange	$\frac{1}{4}$ **pint (full $\frac{1}{2}$ cup) strong tea**

Bring all the ingredients to the boil, simmer for 10 minutes and strain. The tea – which should be very strong but strained immediately on infusion –

can be replaced by a like amount of spirit or liqueur added when the strained syrup cools.

RUM SYRUP

¾ **pint (scant 2 cups) water**
¾ **lb. (1½ cups) sugar**
½ **stick cinnamon**

few seeds coriander
¼ **pint (full ½ cup) rum**

Bring all the ingredients except the rum to the boil and simmer until the syrup thickens. Strain it, let it cool a little and stir in the rum. Brandy and kirsch do well as variations.

FINE SPONGE

Besides making lovely cakes, sponge fingers and Swiss rolls, fine sponge is the basis of many dessert gâteaux. It is made by the whisking method without fat and is also called true sponge to distinguish it from Genoese sponge which has butter in it and Victoria sponge which is made by the creaming method. Some recipes separate the egg whites and beat them stiff before folding them into the rest of the whisked mixture. The basic recipe here follows the British traditional way, whisking the whole eggs. It makes enough for two 8-in. sandwich tins.

BASIC TRUE SPONGE

4 eggs
6 oz. (¾ cup) fine sugar
4 oz. (1 cup) plain flour
for lining tins:

1 oz. (2 tablespoons) butter
½ **oz. (1 tablespoon) cornflour**
  (cornstarch)
½ **oz. (1 tablespoon) fine sugar**

In a large bowl standing over a pan of hot water whisk the eggs and sugar until creamy, pale and stiff enough to take an impression of the whisk and retain it a few moments. With a hand rotary whisk this takes about 15 minutes. Remove the bowl from the heat. Sift half the flour over the mixture and fold it in lightly with a large metal spoon. Sift and fold in the rest of the flour. Brush two 8-in. sandwich (layer) tins with melted butter and dust them with the mixed cornflour and sugar. Pour in the sponge mixture, smooth it and bake near the top of a pre-heated fairly hot oven (375°F., mark 5) for 20–25 minutes.

GÂTEAU PARISIEN

6–8 servings:

1 basic true sponge recipe
(page 143)
2 frangipane cream recipes
(below)
½ pint (1¼ cups) diced fruit

¼ pint (full ½ cup) fruit glaze
(page 123)
1 Italian meringue recipe
(below)
**1 oz. (scant ¼ cup) icing
(confectioners') sugar**

Bake ⅔ of the sponge in a ring mould and ⅓ of it in a sandwich tin to fit the hole in the middle of the ring. Cool on wire racks. Cut the ring in layers ¼–½ in. thick and sandwich them with some of the frangipane cream. Cut the smaller sponge in two layers and fit the bottom layer inside the ring. Mix the finely diced fruit (which can be fresh or candied) with the rest of the frangipane cream, pile it into the middle of the ring and put on the top half of the smaller sponge. Coat all over with thick fruit glaze (page 123). Spread meringue smoothly all over and pipe meringue decorations on top. Sprinkle with icing sugar and return to the oven until the meringue is golden. Serve with a brandy-laced jam sauce.

FRANGIPANE CREAM

**3½ oz. (¾ cup plus 2
tablespoons) flour**
2 whole eggs
3 egg yolks
3½ oz. (scant ½ cup) fine sugar

1 pint (2½ cups) milk
1 oz. (2 tablespoons) butter
**1 oz. (⅓ cup) crushed
macaroons**

Beat together the flour, eggs, yolks and sugar until smooth and creamy. Add the milk and butter and, stirring all the time, cook on gentle heat until nearly boiling. Remove it from the heat, put a ring of wet greaseproof paper on the surface to prevent a skin forming while it cools. Stir in the macaroons when cold.

ITALIAN MERINGUE

**7 oz. (¾ cup plus 2 tablespoons)
sugar**
3 tablespoons (3¾) water
4 egg whites

Boil the sugar and water together until you can pull the syrup to a fine thread with a spoon – that is, at 245°F., 118°C. Leave it to cool a little. Whisk the egg whites until stiff but not dry. Whisking vigorously all the time, gradually add the syrup to the whites.

CARAMEL PISTACHIO GÂTEAU

8 servings:

4 oz. (½ cup) butter	for the filling:
5 oz. (full ½ cup) fine sugar	**4 oz. (½ cup) fine sugar**
4 eggs, beaten	**3 egg yolks**
3 oz. (¾ cup) plain flour	**¼ pint (full ½ cup) milk**
3 oz. (full ⅓ cup) cornflour (cornstarch)	**8 oz. (1 cup) butter**
	for the caramel:
2 teaspoons (2½) baking powder	**6 oz. (¾ cup) sugar**
grated rind 1 lemon	for the decoration:
	3 dozen pistachio nuts

Grease and flour a 3-pint (2-quart) ring mould. Cream the butter and sugar together until pale and fluffy. Add the eggs, a little at a time, beating well. Sift the flour with the cornflour and baking powder, mix in the lemon rind and fold this mixture into the egg mixture. Turn it into the ring mould and bake at 350°F. (mark 4) for about 50 minutes. Turn the cake out and cool it on a wire rack.

For the rich filling, cream the sugar and yolks until thick and pale and add warm milk. Return the mixture to the pan or double boiler and cook over very low heat, stirring, until it is thick enough to coat a wooden spoon. Do not boil it. Cool it. Cream the butter well, gradually beat in the cool egg mixture and beat until fluffy.

For the caramel, set the sugar in a pan over low heat until the sugar melts. When it is turning brown, stir it and continue beating until it is dark golden. Cool it on an oiled slab or greased tin and when it has set crush it.

Slice the cake into three layers. Reserving a little filling for piping, use the rest to sandwich the slices and mask the cake. Cover the cake completely with the broken caramel. Decorate with rosettes of filling and stick the nuts in them. A pretty piece.

CHERRY CREAM CONES

As an alternative to the formal set-piece gâteau, plates of small dessert cakes can make good finishers, attractive and delicious. The cones in this recipe will keep, empty, in an airtight tin for several days. Put in the filling just before serving, certainly not more than an hour before. Peeled seedless grapes or strawberries are good as alternatives to the cherries.

24 cones:
4 oz. (½ cup) butter
5 oz. (scant 1¼ cups) icing
  (confectioners') sugar, sifted
3 egg whites
few drops vanilla essence
4 oz. (1 cup) plain flour
4 tablespoons (5) water

for the filling:
½ pint (1¼ cups) double (heavy)
  cream
¼ pint (full ½ cup) single
  (light) cream
48 stoned cherries
12 cherries on the stem

Cream together the butter and sugar. Beat in the egg whites and essence and then the flour and water. Lightly grease a baking sheet. Drop on to it, spaced well apart, spoonfuls of the batter about 1½ in. across. Flatten them by banging the baking sheet on the table. Bake only one sheet at a time. Bake at 400°F. (mark 6) until the edges turn golden brown and the centres are lightly coloured, about 8 minutes. With a palette knife, quickly remove the discs and shape them into cornets around cream-horn cases. Cool them on a wire rack and carefully slip them off the cases. Whip the double and single cream together until the cream just holds its shape. Just before serving, fill the cone tips with a little cream, add a couple of stoned cherries and a final whirl of cream. Arrange the cones on the serving plate and decorate the pile with cherries on the stem.

RUM CHOCOLATE GÂTEAU

For those who like something rich but reasonably light, here is a gâteau that is popular at a buffet party. The method of making the sponge is a variant of the true sponge recipe. The gâteau is at its best if you eat it the day you make it.

6–8 servings:
for the sponge:
4 eggs, separated
6 oz. (¾ cup) fine sugar
4 oz. (1 cup) self-raising flour
for the filling:
3 oz. (full ⅓ cup) butter
6 oz. (scant 1⅓ cup) icing
  (confectioners') sugar, sifted
1 oz. (¼ cup) preserved ginger

1 oz. (1 square) plain chocolate
4 tablespoons (5) rum
for the topping:
8 oz. (8 squares) plain chocolate
8 oz. (1 cup) unsalted butter
rum to taste
walnuts and preserved ginger
  to decorate

Grease an 8-in. cake tin and line it with greaseproof paper. Beat the egg whites until stiff and very lightly fold in the sugar and beaten egg yolks. Sift the flour into the bowl and fold it carefully into the egg mixture. Pour the

146

mixture into the prepared tin and bake in the centre of a moderate oven until the cake is golden and shrinking from the sides of the tin, about 40 minutes. Turn it out on to a wire rack to cool. To make the filling, chop the ginger finely and grate the chocolate coarsely. Cream the butter and sugar together and stir in the chocolate, ginger and rum. Cut the cake in three layers and sandwich them with the filling. To make the topping, melt the chocolate and butter in a bowl over hot water and add rum to taste (a couple of table-spoons or so). Remove the mixture from the heat to cool until it thickens to a spreading consistency. Spread it roughly with a wet palette knife over the top and sides of the cake and quickly, before it firms, use the rounded end of the palette knife to create freehand 'waves' in it. Decorate quickly too with blanched walnut halves (or other nuts) and little cubes of preserved ginger.

STRUDEL DOUGH

There are many strudel doughs. Baklava dough (pages 160–1) can also be used for strudels. Since all must be paper-thin, cooks in large towns often prefer to buy them at stores, delicatessens, pastry shops or restaurants where they are identified as *strudel* (middle European), *filo* (Greek) or *yufka* (Turkish) doughs. The quantities for the basic strudel dough here give eight sheets, roughly 8 × 16 in. each – enough when filled and rolled up for eight servings.

BASIC STRUDEL DOUGH

8 oz. (2 cups) plain flour
½ teaspoon (⅔) salt
1 egg, beaten
2 tablespoons (2½) olive oil

5 tablespoons (6¼) lukewarm water
1½ oz. (3 tablespoons) butter, melted

Sift together the flour and salt. Combine the egg and oil and put them in the centre of the flour. Add the water gradually, stirring with a fork to make a soft sticky dough. Work the dough until it leaves the sides of the bowl. On a lightly floured surface knead it for about 15 minutes, until it does not stick to hands or board. Put it on a cloth, cover it with a warmed bowl and leave it in a warm place for 1 hour. Warm the rolling pin. Spread a clean tablecloth on the table and lightly but thoroughly dredge it with flour. Roll out the dough into a rectangle about ⅛-in. thick. Lifting the dough on the backs of the hands, stretch it from the centre outwards until all is paper-thin. Trim off the thicker pieces at the edges (the square should be about 32 in. on each side). Leave the dough for 15 minutes, brush it with melted butter, cut it down the centre and cut each half into 4 pieces.

APPLE STRUDEL

Besides apples, popular strudel fillings are stoned cherries or grapes, blue-berries, sliced apricots, plums or rhubarb. Other fillings are of cream cheese combined with eggs, sugar and grated lemon zest, with a little fresh fruit or with raisins.

8 servings:

1 strudel dough recipe (page 147)	**3 oz. (full ⅓ cup) sugar**
4 oz. (⅔ cup) ground almonds	**½ teaspoon (⅔) ground**
2½ lb. cooking apples	**cinnamon**
1½ oz. (¼ cup) seedless raisins	**6 oz. (scant ¾ cup) icing**
1½ oz. (3 tablespoons) currants	**(confectioners') sugar**

Make the dough and cut it in 8 rectangles as described on page 147. Sprinkle it with almonds. Cut the peeled apples wafer-thin and mix them well together with the raisins, currants, fine sugar and cinnamon. Divide the mixture evenly between the 8 pieces of dough and spread it, leaving 1 in. clear on the two short edges and one long edge and 3 in. clear on the other long edge. Fold the three 1-in. edges over the fruit and roll up from the folded-in long side to form a sausage shape. Put the strudel on a greased baking sheet, brush with melted butter and bake in the centre of a pre-heated fairly hot oven (400°F., mark 6) until golden brown, 25–30 minutes. Dust heavily with icing sugar and serve warm or cold.

MERINGUE GÂTEAUX

For the special occasion almost any layered party cake gains a bonus of surprise if one layer of meringue slips in between the layers of puff, sweet shortcrust or fine sponge. One can also build the gâteau with two or three meringue layers on a base of one of these pastries. But the airiest gâteau is surely a pile of thin meringue discs (below) with succulent filling between each. Unless one has a very sweet tooth, it is worth remembering that the meringue itself is very sweet, so adjust the fillings accordingly. They can be the same throughout the gâteau or varied between each layer. About the only crucial point to remember is: if the filling is fruit or in any way moist, spread the meringue disc, thinly but thoroughly, with cream or unsalted butter to stop the juices from softening the meringue.

Fillings. For a non-sweet filling unsalted butter creamed with brandy or rum is good or try 8 oz. (1⅓ cups) chestnut purée beaten smooth with 2 oz. (¼ cup) butter and 2 tablespoons (2½) kirsch or maraschino. For a sweeter chestnut butter cream one can substitute *marrons glacés*, pounded or sieved, for some or all of the purée. Other good fillings are chocolate cream sauce (page 136), Chiboust cream (page 137), French pastry cream (page 137), Chantilly cream (page 139), the almond cream of gâteau Pithiviers (page 139) or nut honey butter (page 140). And any of the fillings can incorporate or be sprinkled with chopped nuts, chopped candied fruits or chocolate vermicelli.

Finishing. With the meringue discs mounted, the fillings can be smoothed off around the side and the whole of the gâteau covered with a glacé icing (page 141). Otherwise, only the top layer need be iced and the sides can be piped with whipped cream, thick Chantilly cream or other piping mixtures.

MERINGUE DISCS

For two 8-in. discs take 4 egg whites and 8 oz. (1 cup) fine sugar. Whisk the whites until they are stiff. Gradually add in half the sugar, whisking until stiff again. Fold in the rest of the sugar. Draw two 8-in. circles on silicone (non-stick) paper and put the paper on a baking sheet. Even better, place the paper on a damp flat board. A good way to spread the meringue on the paper is to pipe it, starting around the circumference of the circle and spiralling into the centre. Smooth it with a spatula. Spread half the meringue mixture evenly on each circle. Bake in the coolest part of the slowest oven until dry, about 1½ hours. Cool thoroughly on a wire base before removing the paper.

CROQUEMBOUCHE OF MERINGUES

If *croquembouche* really comes from *croque en bouche* (crunch in the mouth), the meringue *croquembouche* is surely the most typical example. For a good party piece, make about four dozen round meringue shells about 1 in. in diameter, using a plain piping nozzle. Make them in different colours and flavours. Glaze their flat sides with sugar cooked to the crack stage (270°F., 132°C.) and stick them together in pairs. Arrange the pairs in a pyramid or cone, distributing the colours in some sort of pattern, using more of the glazing sugar to fix them firmly. Dip preserved cherries, drained, or glacé cherries in the glazing sugar and decorate the pyramid with them as you fancy.

One can make a border for the *croquembouche* with meringues too. Make them again in different colours and flavours – say white with vanilla essence, green with peppermint and red with strawberry essence. Stick them together in pairs by glazing their flat sides with the cooked sugar. Arrange them around the dish or platter, using more sugar to fix them in position. The same border can be used without the *croquembouche* of course. Simply fill up the centre of the dish with Chantilly cream (page 139) flavoured with fruit juice or liqueur and decorate with berry fruits or any other suitable filling.

VACHERINS

The French make elegant desserts called vacherins either with meringue or with almond paste. They vary the shapes, sometimes using the meringue or paste in discs, sometimes forming it into rings which are mounted, one on top of another, around the edge of a pastry base. The centre is then piled with any of the fillings suitable for meringue gâteaux (above). Queen Marie-Antoinette liked vacherins and used to make them herself. The recipe I give for an ice-cream vacherin below is one I enjoyed at a gastronomic weekend at the Imperial Hotel in Torquay, Devon. For a ring-type meringue vacherin pipe two circles of meringue 9 in. in diameter on to silicone (non-stick) paper and cook them in the slowest oven until they are quite dry. Mount one ring on top of the other and coat the double ring with more meringue. Decorate the top and the outside with fancy pipings of meringue. Sprinkle with fine sugar and again dry it out in the slowest oven. When the ring has cooled fix it, with sugar cooked to the crack stage (270°F., 132°C.), on to a 9-in. base of choux or other pastry. It is now ready for the chosen filling and any decoration one wishes to add.

Here is the Imperial's *Vacherin glacé aux raisins sec.* (*Illustrated*)

4 servings:

2 meringue discs (page 149)
2 oz. ($\frac{1}{3}$ cup) seedless raisins
2 tablespoons (2$\frac{1}{2}$) rum
**$\frac{1}{4}$ pint (1$\frac{1}{4}$ cups) double
  (heavy) cream, whipped**

**$\frac{1}{2}$ pint (1$\frac{1}{4}$ cups) soft coffee ice
  cream**
strawberries or
**2 oz. ($\frac{1}{3}$ cup) blanched almonds
  toasted golden**

Chill the meringue discs. Soak the raisins in the rum for at least an hour. Mix them and 2 tablespoons of the whipped cream with the ice cream and spread the mixture quickly between the two discs. Put the vacherin immediately into the home freezer or the coldest part of the refrigerator to set hard. Twenty minutes before serving, pipe the whipped cream on top and sides and decorate with the strawberries or almonds and any extra ice cream if desired. Replace in refrigerator until required.

some exotics

In both figurative and literal senses of the word, the most truly exotic dessert I call to mind is, I suppose, the Chinese delicacy, bird's nest. Dietetically it is predigested protein processed from seaweed by Pacific Ocean petrels. As a sweet, it is soaked in tepid water for three hours, washed, simmered for two hours and served with sugar.

Modern transport and food-handling make almost everything available everywhere. But even before that many ingredients of our puddings were so familiar that they no longer seemed exotic, particularly the spices from the hot countries. Most of them come from flowers. Cloves are flower buds, saffron is the stigmas of a purple crocus, tamarind from a seed pod and vanilla from an orchid, not to mention the flower seeds, from aniseed to poppy and sesame. I have mentioned flower fritters in chapter 8.

Flavourings are also made from the flowers themselves. In Shakespeare's day sweet waters, distilled or infused at home, were made from the reputedly magical elder flower, damask rose, orange blossom and many other flowers. They were much used in cooking, particularly in custards. And I like a later recipe, from the 1747 edition of Hannah Glasse's book, for a marmalade of eggs. It uses 24 eggs 'beaten for an hour' with 1 lb. (2 cups) sugar, 1 oz. (3 tablespoons) pounded almonds and 4 spoonfuls of orange-flower water. The mixture is brought to custard consistency over a slow fire. Nowadays some of these flavourings – rose water and orange-blossom water, for instance – can be bought. These flower waters are still used in west European pastrymaking and confectionery. From the Balkans eastward they add fragrance to all sorts of desserts, sweetmeats and drinks – baklavas, halvas, sweet rice dishes, Turkish delight, fruit salads and compotes. They are best used sparingly – say, 1 teaspoon (1¼) to a rice pudding or 2 tablespoons (2½) to a syrup of 1 lb. (2 cups) sugar in ½ pint (1¼ cups) water.

For flower waters or desserts use flowers freshly picked in the cool of the morning and flowers which have not had the perfume bred out of them.

Choose small violets – wild ones are best – and lilac trimmed of all stems and with roses, marigolds or carnations take only the petals, trimmed of any white parts.

ROSE-WATER—VIOLET-WATER

Mash $\frac{3}{4}$ lb. damask rose petals (or violets) in a mortar or an electric blender and add them to $1\frac{1}{4}$ pints (full 3 cups) boiling water. Immediately remove it from the heat and cover tightly – 'so close that none of the virtue may exhale', as one old recipe says. After 12 hours add 1 lb. (2 cups) fine sugar and cook in a lidded double boiler over simmering water until the sugar dissolves. Keep covered until cool. Strain it through muslin and bottle it.

ROSE HONEY

This is a recipe from Nell Gwynne's day. Pour 3 pints ($3\frac{3}{4}$) boiling water over $\frac{1}{2}$ lb. trimmed petals, cover and leave for 12 hours. Strain the liquid through fine cloth and when it is clear add it to 5 lb. honey and boil until it thickens.

CARNATION SYRUP

Pour 3 pints ($3\frac{3}{4}$) boiling water over 1 lb. carnation petals and cover for 8 hours. Heat again, strain through fine cloth and squeeze the petals well. To the liquid add 1 lb. fresh petals, infuse for 8 hours, strain and press. Add $1\frac{1}{2}$ lb. sugar to the liquid and boil it to a syrup.

ROSE PETAL PRESERVE

For a preserve liquid (enough to make a sauce for puddings or ice cream), barely cover the petals with cold water and simmer to a pulp. Weigh the pulp, add an equal weight of sugar, boil until it sets and pot as jam. Norman Douglas in his *Venus in the Kitchen or Love's Cookery Book* gives a similar concoction of red carnations which are 'useful for people of cold temperament'.

SUGAR-FROSTED FLOWERS (*Illustrated*)

For edible decorations on cold desserts, brush violets, lilac flowers, rose petals or mint leaves on both sides with lightly beaten egg white. Dust them with fine sugar and dry them off on silicone paper or waxed paper – in the sun or in a very slow oven with the door ajar. Store them between layers of silicone paper in airtight jars.

LILAC MERINGUE

4 servings:

2 egg whites
4 oz. ($\frac{1}{2}$ cup) fine sugar
$\frac{1}{2}$ pint (1$\frac{1}{4}$ cups) double (heavy)
  cream, whipped

4 tablespoons (5) framboise
  brandy
$\frac{1}{2}$ lb. raspberries
sugar-frosted or crystallized
  lilac flowers

On greaseproof paper draw a circle 7 in. across, oil the paper and put it on a baking sheet. Make a meringue with the egg whites and sugar and, with about half of it, make a thin disc on the circle (page 149). With the rest, pipe small rosettes on to the paper. Dry off the meringue in the slowest oven for about an hour. Lift the rosettes and disc carefully off the paper with a palette knife and cool them on a wire rack. Spread half the whipped cream, laced with the raspberry eau-de-vie (or with crème de framboise if you prefer it sweeter), over the disc. Set the rosettes around the rim. Make a cone in the centre with the rest of the cream. Arrange the raspberries around it and cover the cone with lilac flowers (or other small frosted flowers or petals).

LAVENDER PASTE

For a sugar paste to use with pastry, pound or blend lavender flowers (or white lilac, violets or petals) with 2$\frac{1}{2}$ times their weight of fine sugar. Store in sealed jars. Also, one may do as the Turks do – dry them off in uncovered glass jars in the sun each day until the top of the mixture is crystallized.

PEKING DUST

Many of these flower recipes were widely used in England until a couple of centuries ago. Now they are more truly exotic to us. So are many sweets from Asia and the Pacific – for instance, Peking dust, a recipe which first came to me from my friend Rebecca Hsu, well-known cookery expert of Hong Kong.

4 servings:

1 lb. chestnuts, in shell
$\frac{1}{2}$ oz. (1 tablespoon) sugar

$\frac{1}{2}$ pint (1$\frac{1}{4}$ cups) cream, whipped
4 oz. ($\frac{2}{3}$ cup) glacé cherries

Boil the chestnuts until they burst, shell and skin them while still warm. When cold purée them with the sugar. Divide into 4 individual bowls, pipe on whipped cream and decorate with cherries. Garnish with spun sugar (page 154).

SPUN SUGAR

8 oz. (1 cup) sugar   **½ oz. (2 tablespoons) glucose**
¼ pint (full ½ cup) water

Oil a wooden stick – a rolling pin or long wooden spoon handle will do – and cover the table with a clean sheet of paper. Gently heat the sugar, water and glucose together until the sugar has dissolved. Boil to 300°F. (149°C)., brushing down any sugar splashes on the pan sides with a pastry brush dipped in cold water. At 300°F. immediately stand the pan in cold water for a few minutes. Holding the rolling pin over the paper, dip a fork in the syrup and swing it quickly back and forth above the rolling pin. The higher the swings, the longer the threads that fall on the rolling pin. For a halo or ring of spun sugar, swing the fork round and round a shallow cone of silicone paper.

ALMOND TEA

The name tea is somewhat misleading but the Chinese drink it like tea in cups, often between courses of a long feast. For Western tastes it is also delicious cold.

4 servings:
1 oz. (3 tablespoons) rice   **2¼ pints (5⅔ cups) water**
½ pint (1¼ cups) skinned   **3 oz. (full ⅓ cup) sugar**
   almonds

Soak the rice in cold water for 15 minutes and drain it. Mix it with the almonds and ¼ pint (full ½ cup) water and put the mixture through a blender for 4 minutes. Add the mixture and sugar to the rest of the water in a pan. Bring it to the boil, reduce heat and simmer, covered, for 30 minutes.

WON TONS

Delightful Chinese mouthfuls, dessert *won tons* are paper-thin paste wrapped around ½ teaspoonful of sweet filling (page 155) and then deep-fried in oil at 375°F. (191°C.) or cooked in boiling water and later pan-fried. The paste is best bought at Chinese stores or restaurants but it can be made with 4 oz. (1 cup) plain flour, a pinch of salt and 1 egg. Drop the egg into the sifted flour and salt and knead thoroughly until the dough is quite elastic. Leave it under a damp cloth for 30 minutes. Then on a floured board and with a floured roller roll it out paper-thin. It should be thin enough to give a couple of dozen 3-in. squares. Keep the squares covered with a damp cloth until use.

The Chinese fold these wrappings in various ways. One of the simplest is to have the corner of a square pointing towards you and place ½ teaspoon of filling about ¼ in. from the corner. Dab the corner with water, fold it over with the filling and press the corner down. Fold again in the same direction so that the fold meets the far corner, which you dab with water and press down. Fold the side corners in so that they just overlap and press them together with a dab of water.

To cook *won tons*, lower them into deep hot oil, a few at a time, until golden. Drain and serve. Reheat the oil between batches. Or drop them into boiling water, bring the water to the boil again and lift out the *won tons* when they float. Drain them, shallow-fry them and serve them with a honey-and-ginger sauce as a dip.

SWEET WON TON FILLINGS

Small pieces of fruit flesh – melon, papaya or pineapple particularly – dipped in ginger syrup are good. Or mix ½ lb. dried fruits with 1 oz. (⅓ cup) sesame seeds and 3 tablespoons (3¾) honey. The dried fruits can be currants, raisins, sultanas, dates (pitted), figs or prunes – or a mixture – finely chopped, pounded or ground.

ITALIAN ALMOND DESSERT

The Italians, the world's leading exporters of almonds, make many desserts with them. The *budino di mandorle* here can be varied by the inclusion of rice or rice flour or by leaving out the egg yolks and the candied fruit.

4–6 servings:

½ lb. (1⅓ cups) peeled almonds
6 oz. (¾ cup) fine sugar
4 eggs
4–5 tablespoons (5–5¼) grappa
  or brandy
1 oz. (¼ cup) finely chopped
candied orange peel
1 oz. (¼ cup) finely chopped
  candied apricot
1 oz. (1 tablespoon) butter
2 tablespoons (2½) fine
  breadcrumbs

Pound the almonds finely with nearly all the sugar and blend in gradually 1 beaten egg. Beat 3 egg yolks with the grappa and add the finely-chopped fruit. Add the fruit mixture to the almonds, blend well and fold in 3 stiffly whisked egg whites. Butter a baking or soufflé dish, dust it with breadcrumbs and spoon in the mixture. Stand the dish in a baking tin of water and bake in a moderate oven until the surface begins to colour, about 30–40 minutes. Serve cold, sprinkled with sugar.

TORTA DI NOCI

A variant of the almond pudding, this regional Italian dish specifically excludes the dominant almonds. It can be made with only one kind of nut but gains subtlety if one mixes say, walnuts, pistachios, pine nuts and hazel nuts.

4 servings:

5 eggs, separated
8 oz. (2 cups) mixed nuts
8 oz. (1 cup) fine sugar
8 oz. (8 squares) bitter
   chocolate, grated

2 oz. ($\frac{1}{2}$ cup) fine-chopped
   candied orange peel
1 teaspoon ($1\frac{1}{4}$) salt
$\frac{1}{4}$ pint (full $\frac{1}{2}$ cup) marsala
2 good slices bread
2 oz. ($\frac{1}{4}$ cup) butter

Beat the egg yolks and pound the nuts. Combine them well with the sugar, chocolate, peel, salt, and marsala. Crumb the bread and fry the crumbs lightly in butter. Butter a shallow ovenproof dish and spread the crumbs over the butter. Whisk the egg whites stiffly and fold them into the nut mixture. Pour the mixture into the dish and bake in a moderate oven (350°F., mark 4) for 30 minutes. Serve the tart hot or cold.

COCONUTS

Coconut, coconut cream and coconut milk are widely used in tropical desserts. Fresh coconuts are best but dried coconut and butter-like slabs of coconut cream can be bought.

Grated coconut
The white flesh of the coconut, with its brown skin removed, is grated and combined with taro and other flours, mashed bananas or papaya, and eggs in puddings, pies, fritters, custards and mousses. A Pacific island dessert has peeled bananas with slits in their top sides stuffed with grated coconut and a little sugar. They are cooked in shallow simmering water for 45 minutes and served cold with chilled coconut cream.

Coconut cream
Add to the grated flesh of two large coconuts just enough hot (not boiling) water to cover it. Let it stand for 30 minutes, wrap it in muslin and press out all the juice. Stand the juice in a cool place until the cream rises to the top and skim off the cream. If you use dessicated coconut let it infuse in the water for 1 hour. It can be heated but it loses its creaminess if it boils.

156

Coconut milk

The juice of the grated coconut once pressed (as in the first stage of making coconut cream) is sometimes called thick coconut milk. Thin coconut milk comes when the same grated coconut is re-soaked and again pressed, once or twice more. Thick and thin can of course be mixed. The pressed coconut can be eaten with a sweet sauce on its own or mixed into rice or tapioca puddings.

MALAYSIAN SARIKAUJI

4 servings:

4 eggs   **1 pint (2½ cups) coconut milk**
4 oz. (½ cup) sugar   **1 tablespoon (1¼) rose water**

Beat the eggs and sugar together until pale and fluffy. Beat in the coconut milk, little by little, and the rose-water. Pour the mixture into a buttered basin or mould, cover with greaseproof paper and steam until set, about 1 hour. Serve chilled.

RUSSIAN PASKHA

A traditional Easter dessert, *paskha* makes a wonderful party dish. Correctly, it is served with cream and slices of *koulich*, a rich yeast currant cake sometimes called Easter bread. This recipe needs no cooking but, if it is to be kept for a couple of days, the mixture can be brought almost to the boil and then cooled before it goes into the mould.

4–6 servings:

1 lb. (2 cups) curd (cottage) cheese   **grated rind 1 orange**
4 oz. (½ cup) butter   **2 oz. (⅓ cup) sultanas**
4 oz. (½ cup) vanilla sugar   **maraschino cherries**
2 egg yolks   **angelica**
¼ pint (full ½ cup) double (heavy) cream

Hang the cheese in muslin overnight or press it to make it as dry as possible. Cream the butter, sugar and eggs together until fluffy. Sieve the cheese and beat it into the butter, little by little. Stir in the cream, orange rind and sultanas. Line a basin with butter muslin, fill it and press the mixture well down. Cover it with a weighted plate and chill, preferably in a refrigerator, overnight. Unmould and serve decorated with cherries and angelica.

INDIAN JELLEBIS

Also called *jalebis* and *jilbis*, these fritters are deep-fried in *ghee* (clarified butter) or oil. They are often tinted by adding colouring to the syrup – in India *haldi* or *kesar* but any edible vegetable colouring will do. The Spaniards enjoy a breakfast fritter, *churros*, made in much the same way. They are made of choux paste piped into hot deep fat where they puff up in long curls. Then they are drained and sprinkled with sugar.

4 servings:

1 lb. (2 cups) sugar
1 pint (2½ cups) water
4 oz. (1 cup) plain flour

½ teaspoon (⅔) baking powder
1 oz. (3 tablespoons) ground pistachio nuts

Boil the sugar and water to a rather heavy syrup and keep it warm. Sift the flour and baking powder together and add enough water to give a batter of the consistency of thin cream. Heat the oil to 380–385°F. (193°–196°C.). Pour the batter into a funnel, closing the bottom of it with your finger. Over the oil, release the finger and 'draw' concentric circles or figures of 8 with the batter in the oil, closing the funnel's outlet when enough has poured. When the fritters are golden brown, remove them and drop them into the syrup for 5 minutes. Take them out, drain them and sprinkle with the pistachio nuts.

HALVAS

Halvas are popular from the Spice Islands to the Balkans, where sweets are apt to be very sweet. Scores of recipes include variously lentils, potatoes or different meals or flours, sometimes adding eggs or milk evaporated until it is a thick paste (called *khoa* in Tamil and *kova* in Hindi). Halvas are eaten hot or cold. My first recipe is from Pakistan but is really international. The papaya halva illustrates the fruit and vegetable halvas. The best alternative I have found, if the delectable papaya is not at hand, is ripe charentais melon.

SEMOLINA HALVA

4–6 servings:

4 oz. (½ cup) sugar
¼ pint (full ½ cup) water
4 oz. (½ cup) butter
4 oz. (9½ tablespoons) semolina
½ teaspoon (⅔) ground cardamom seeds

2 oz. (⅓ cup) seedless raisins
2 oz. (⅓ cup) pistachio nuts
2 oz. (⅓ cup) almonds
½ oz. (⅔) ground cinnamon

158

Dissolve the sugar in water in a pan, boiling until it begins to thicken. Remove it from the heat. Melt the butter and lightly fry the semolina in it. Add the cardamom to the semolina. Pour in the syrup, add the raisins and finely chopped nuts and stir over low heat until the mixture thickens. Beat it vigorously with a wooden spoon and pour into wet moulds. Turn out and serve sprinkled with cinnamon.

PAPAYA HALVA

4–6 servings:

¾ lb. (3 cups) diced papaya flesh

½ pint (2½ cups) milk

¾ lb. (1½ cups) sugar

¾ lb. (1½ cups) clarified butter, melted

1 teaspoon (1¼) saffron

Add the papaya to the milk and bring it gently to the boil. Add the sugar, stirring constantly, and then the melted butter, little by little. Add the saffron and stir until the mixture is thick and leaves the sides of the pan cleanly. (Another test for halvas is to cool a spoonful on a saucer for a couple of minutes, when the mixture should be firm.) Pour the halva into wet moulds. Turn out when cool and set.

SWEET POTATO DESSERTS

The hot-country people seem more enterprising in using vegetables in desserts. The Indians and Malayans put tomatoes, potatoes and beetroots into halva and carrots into *murabba*. The Indonesians make two desserts with sweet potatoes, which are of course not related to the ordinary potato.

One, called *pilus*, combines 1 pint (2½ cups) of mashed cooked sweet potato with 2 tablespoons (2½) flour, 1 egg and 1½ tablespoons (2) brown sugar. Formed into small balls and deep-fried they are good hot with a jam or honey sauce or cold with thick cream.

The other is *Kolak ubi* which the Indonesian Embassy in London first introduced to me, pointing out incidentally that pumpkin or marrow can be used in place of the sweet potatoes. Take 1 pint (2½ cups) of diced sweet potatoes and cook them in 1½ pints (3¾ cups) of coconut milk (page 157) with a 1-in. stick of cinnamon, a clove and a pinch of salt. Take out the cinnamon and clove and serve the sweet potatoes in the milk, hot or cold.

KATJANG HIDJAU

This sweet from Indonesia uses Chinese green peas, which are not difficult to find in specialist food shops in the west. Good full-cream cow's milk can substitute for the coconut milk.

4 servings:

1 pint (2¼ cups) Chinese green peas
water

1 oz. (2 tablespoons) sugar
1 pint (2¼ cups) coconut milk
1 knob green ginger

Cover the peas with water and cook them over gentle heat for 30 minutes, adding boiling water to keep them covered if need be. Add the sugar, coconut milk and the ginger, sliced, and cook for 5 minutes more.

SERIKAYA

Another Indonesian dessert is a banana pudding flavoured with powdered dried vanilla pod.

4 servings:

1 egg
vanilla pod, powdered
1 oz. (2 tablespoons) sugar

½ pint (1¼ cups) milk
3 bananas

Beat the egg with the powdered vanilla pod – about an inch of it, or to taste. Stir in the sugar and milk. Add the sliced bananas and steam the mixture gently in its serving dish until it sets, 20–30 minutes.

BAKLAVA

Throughout eastern Mediterranean lands baklava is a top sweet for parties. Persians feature it at their new year, Aide Noruz, at weddings and like occasions. Jewish communities serve it on every festival. Turks and Greeks enjoy it – and they also use the paper-thin pastry to make little turnovers, savoury as well as sweet. Baklava pastry can be bought in cities and large towns in Britain, the United States and other western countries and strudel pastry, a quite satisfactory substitute, can also be bought. The professionals make it so much thinner than most home cooks that two buttered layers should be used for every one layer in the following recipe if bought pastry is used.

160

6–8 servings

12 oz. (3 cups) flour	**½ tablespoon (⅔) ground**
1 teaspoon (1¼) salt	**cardamom seeds**
1 tablespoon (1¼) olive oil	for the syrup:
½ pint (1¼ cups) lukewarm	**8 oz. (1 cup) sugar**
water	**⅓ pint (1 cup) honey**
1¼ lb. (2½ cups) unsalted butter	**½ pint (1¼ cups) water**
12 oz. (2 cups) chopped walnuts	**juice 1 lemon**

Grease a baking tin – say, 12 × 15 × 2 in. Sift the flour and salt together and stir in the oil. Add enough water for a firm dough, knead well and let stand 1 hour. Roll it out on a floured cloth as thinly as possible, and then, lifting it on the back of the hands, stretch it paper-thin. Cut it in sheets to fit your tin. Place one sheet in the tin, brush with melted butter, and add two more sheets, brushing each with butter. Sprinkle with nuts and a pinch of cardamom. Continue alternating buttered sheets with nuts and spice and finish with 3 buttered sheets. Cut into diagonal sections across the pan and cut intersecting diagonals to form diamonds. Cook in a moderate oven until golden, about 45 minutes. Meantime, boil the sugar, honey, water and lemon juice together on medium heat for 20–25 minutes. When the baklava is cooked, drain off its butter and while it is still hot pour the syrup over it. Leave it to cool in the tin.

FRUIT SALADS

Watermelons are not normally regarded as gourmet fare but what they lack in delicacy of flavour they certainly make up in that wondrous rosy-pink flesh. They also come large, which is why you can often buy half of one and little boys and girls get it by the slice from my favourite greengrocer on hot summer Saturdays. So do I, as a thirst-quencher when watching cricket. But use it cunningly and it becomes a centre-piece fruit salad as subtle to eat as it is delightful to the eye.

SHIH CHIN KUO PIN

The Chinese have a way with watermelons, which in their country come in great variety. They cut them in half, lengthwise, and take out the seeds. Then they cut out the flesh in chunks, as large as possible, but carefully leave around the cut shell rim a lining of the flesh, cut smoothly, for its gorgeous colour. Then make the filling (which makes it special). With a small scoop, make little balls of the melon flesh and put them into a large

161

bowl. Add lychees, mangosteens, kumquats, loquats, guavas – oh, any of those wonderful tropical fruits you fancy. And for further texture contrast add crisp cubes of apples or pears (dipped in lemon juice immediately they are cut). Add too, stoned prunes (if you have some marinating in brandy in your store cupboard). Add sugar syrup, blended with cinnamon to taste and a little white wine. Pile the mixture into the melon shell and chill the lot in the refrigerator for a couple of hours before serving it.

RUDJAK TEGAL

Here is another fruit salad, a spicy Indonesian one exploiting vegetables as well as fruits and using the oriental penchant for contrasts – hot and smooth, sweet and sour. It has a sugar syrup rather thicker than that suggested for the fruit salads in chapter 9, the sort of syrup widely used with sweets and pastries throughout the East. Not here but for other uses – to soak, dunk or sprinkle desserts, for instance – it is often flavoured with spices and/or rose water or orange-blossom water – in a proportion of approximately 2 tablespoons ($2\frac{1}{2}$) to the $\frac{1}{2}$ pint ($1\frac{1}{4}$ cups) of syrup.

The tamarind, if you can get it or make it, is much the best of the alternatives (vinegar or lemon juice being the others) given in this recipe. It is a sweet-sour syrup prepared from tamarind pods and is widely sold, ready-made, in the East and around the Mediterranean (by chemists in Italy, for example). In Britain and other western countries Indian shops sell dried tamarind pods, called *tamarindo*, which can be soaked overnight using 1 lb. pods to $1\frac{1}{2}$ pints ($3\frac{3}{4}$ cups) water. Then sieve the pods back into their soaking water, strain and press the mixture through cloth. Add sugar to taste – 1 lb. for the sour tamarind needed here – and let it dissolve. Simmer the syrup for 5 minutes and it will keep in screw-top bottles.

4–6 servings:

for the syrup:
1 lb. (2 cups) brown sugar
1 pint ($2\frac{1}{2}$ cups) water
1 oz. (3 tablespoons) ground peanuts
1 teaspoon ($1\frac{1}{4}$) salt
1 teaspoon ($1\frac{1}{4}$) crushed chilli
1 tablespoon ($1\frac{1}{4}$) lemon juice, vinegar or tamarind

for the salad:
1 cup ($1\frac{1}{4}$) shredded carrots
3 cups ($3\frac{3}{4}$) eating apples, cooking apples, pears and cucumbers, mixed and diced

Dissolve the sugar in the water, bring it to the boil and boil it gently for 8 minutes, stirring in the peanuts, salt and chilli. As the mixture cools, stir in the lemon juice, vinegar or tamarind. Trim and scrape the carrots and grate

162

them, coarsely, into the syrup. Estimate the fruits and cucumber to give about equal amounts of each. As soon as each is peeled and diced, stir it at once into the cooled syrup. Chill the salad for 2 hours before serving it. Serve it with chilled coconut cream (page 156), ideally, or with whipped cream – unflavoured so that you get the maximum from the subtleties of the salad.

ORANGES À LA TURQUE (*Illustrated*)

So common that we no longer regard them as exotics, oranges come to us in Britain all the year round, from Spain, Morocco, California, Israel, South Africa and Australia and other countries. Even Chinese kumquats, the plum-size dwarfs which are wonderful preserved whole in heavy syrup, come from Morocco. And then there are their cousins from the Caribbean overflowing with tropical flavour – the ortanique (sweet orange crossed with tangerine) and the lumpy ugli (a grapefruit-mandarin cross). Together they contribute a vast variety to desserts, sweet sauces and other dishes, each to be enjoyed for its particular character and in its best season. For *Oranges à la turque* good varieties available in Britain and America are Valencias, Jaffa shamoutis and, supremely, the navel, a seedless all-year type so called because of the odd little bud on the top.

8 servings:

8 large navel oranges	**1 lb. (2 cups) fine sugar**
water	**3 cloves**

Peel the oranges over a bowl to catch any escaping juice, leaving them whole but removing all white pith and the exposed skins of the segments. Finely cut the rinds free from white pith from 4 orange peels. Cut into julienne strips, matchstick thin. Put the strips of rind in a pan with water enough to cover them and cook them with gentleness, covered, until tender. Strain them, saving the liquid, and let them cool. Add the caught orange juice to the strained water and make the liquid up to $\frac{1}{2}$ pint ($1\frac{1}{4}$ cups) with more water. Dissolve the sugar in this mixture, add the cloves, bring it to the boil and boil it gently until it is caramel coloured. Remove it from the heat and thoroughly stir in 3 tablespoons ($3\frac{3}{4}$) cold water. Arrange the oranges on a flat serving dish, spoon over them the caramel syrup and leave them in a cool place for several hours. Turn them once or twice, spooning the syrup over them and top them with the julienne strips before the last spooning. Serve them with knife, fork and spoon – the spoon because the syrup is too lovely to miss.

Bibliography

Allen-Gray, Dorothy, *Fare Exchange*, Faber, 1963

Athenaeus, *The Deipnosophists*, with English translation by Charles Burton Gulick, Heinemann (London) and Harvard University Press, 1941

Austin, Thomas (Ed), *Two Fifteenth Century Cookery Books*, Oxford University Press, 1964

Bar-David, Molly Lyons, *Jewish Cooking for Pleasure*, Hamlyn, 1965

Cheng, F. T., *Musings of a Chinese Gourmet*, Hutchinson, 1962

David, Elizabeth, *Italian Food*, Macdonald, 1965

Day, Avanelle, and Stuckey, Lillie, *Cooking for Flavour with Spices and Herbs*, Collins, 1968

Douglas, Norman (Ed), *Venus in the Kitchen or Love's Cookery Book*, Pilaff Bey, Heinemann, 1952

Drummond, J. C., and Wilbraham, A. (revised by Dorothy Hollingsworth), *The Englishman's Food, a History of Five Centuries of English Diet*, Jonathan Cape, 1957

Ellison, J. Audrey (Ed), *Great Scandinavian Cook Book*, Allen & Unwin, 1966

Escoffier, Auguste, *Ma Cuisine*, Paul Hamlyn, 1965

Frazer, James G., *The Golden Bough*, Macmillan, 1911

Glasse, Hannah, *The Art of Cookery Made Plain and Easy*, T. Longman, 1796

Good Housekeeping's Cookery Book, 1966, and *Good Housekeeping's Cookery Encyclopaedia*, 1964, Ebury Press

Hutchins, Sheila, *English Recipes and Others*. Methuen, 1967

Hutchison, R. (revised by V. H. Mottram and George Graham), *Food and the Principles of Dietetics*, Edward Arnold, 1956

Larousse Gastronomique, Paul Hamlyn, 1965

Mayer-Browne, Elisabeth, *Austrian Cooking for You*, Bles, 1969

Mayda, Maideh, *In a Persian Kitchen*, Charles E. Tuttle, 1960

McNeill, F. Marian, *The Scots' Kitchen*, Blackie, 1963

Roden, Claudia, *A Book of Middle Eastern Food*, Nelson, 1968

Roussin, René, *Royal Menus*, Hammond, 1960

Samuelson, M. K., *Sussex Recipe Book*, Country Life, 1937

Simon, André L., *André Simon's Guide to Good Food and Wine*, Collins, 1963

Slater, Mary, *Cooking the Caribbean Way*, Paul Hamlyn, 1965

Taglienti, Maria Luisa, *The Italian Cookbook*, Spring, 1964

Trethewy, Yvonne, *Successful Cooking*, Country Life, 1961

comparative cookery measures

It is not simple to convert with absolute accuracy measurements for the kitchen. Generally speaking, absolute accuracy is not required, except when making cakes or pastries. Throughout this book both British and American measurements have been used and, as far as possible, ingredients have been measured in cups and tablespoons for easy conversion.

Fortunately for the cook, British and American solid weights are equivalent; but this does not always mean that the British housewife can readily understand American measurements or *vice versa*. In the United States the average housewife has her set of measuring spoons and cups. In Britain this is never so general, although most housewives do have a measuring cup or jug.

The British measuring cup used in this book is the British Standard Institute's Cup which gives a $\frac{1}{2}$-pint measure, the equivalent to 10 fluid ounces (it is the size of the average British breakfastcup or tumbler). The American standard cup is equal to the American $\frac{1}{2}$-pint, which is equivalent to 8 fluid ounces.

All spoon measurements are level unless otherwise specified.

Throughout this book British measurements are given first; the American equivalent follows, where necessary, in brackets.

Conversion of measures into British and American measures

Exact measurements are, of course, not possible, and if applied in the kitchen would require all housewife-cooks to be also mathematicians, which most of us are not. The best, therefore, is the nearest approximate.

EXACT MEASUREMENTS

1 kilogram (kg) = 2.2 lb.   1 litre (l.) = 1.8 pints

166

APPROXIMATE MEASUREMENTS USED

1 lb. = 0.5 kg. or 500 grams 1 gallon = 4.5 litres
8 oz. = 240 grams   1 quart = 1.125 litres ($1\frac{1}{8}$ litres)
4 oz. = 120 grams   1 pint = 0.5 litres
1 oz. = 30 grams $\frac{1}{2}$ pint = 0.25 litres
            $\frac{1}{4}$ pint = 0.125 litres ($\frac{1}{8}$ litre)

vintage chart

Year	Claret	Burgundy	White Burgundy	Sauterne	Loire	Rhone	Rhine	Moselle	Champagne	Port
1945	7	5	–	6	–	7	–	–	5	7
1946	1	1	–	2	–	3	–	–	–	–
1947	5	6	–	6	–	6	–	–	5	7
1948	5	5	–	5	–	4	–	–	–	7
1949	6	5	–	6	–	7	–	–	5	–
1950	5	3	–	6	–	5	–	–	–	6
1951	0	1	–	2	–	2	–	–	–	–
1952	6	5	4	5	–	6	–	–	6	–
1953	6	4	3	5	–	6	7	6	6	–
1954	4	3	1	2	–	3	1	1	–	6
1955	6	4	4	7	–	6	5	4	6	7
1956	0	0	0	2	–	3	1	1	–	–
1957	5	5	5	4	–	6	4	4	–	–
1958	5	3	4	5	–	4	4	4	–	6
1959	6	6	5	6	6	6	7	7	7	–
1960	4	1	1	3	2	6	2	2	–	7
1961	7	6	6	6	5	7	5	4	7	–
1962	6	5	6	6	4	6	3	3	6	–
1963	1	2	3	0	1	2	3	2	–	7
1964	6	7	7	4	6	6	6	7	7	–
1965	1	1	2	0	1	2	1	1	–	–
1966	6	6	7	5	5	6	6	6	–	7
1967	6	5	6	5	6	6	5	4	–	6
1968	1	1	3	0	3	2	3	2	–	–
1969	5	7	7	6	7	5	5	5	–	–

0 = no good   7 = the best

index

170

The International Wine and Food Society

The International Wine and Food Society was founded in 1933 by André L. Simon, C.B.E., as a world-wide non-profit-making society.

The first of its various aims has been to bring together and serve all who believe that a right understanding of wine and food is an essential part of personal contentment and health; and that an intelligent approach to the pleasures and problems of the table offers far greater rewards than the mere satisfaction of appetite.

For information about the Society apply to the Secretary,

Marble Arch House, 44 Edgware Road, London W2